Whisper
IN THE
STORM

A STORY OF GOD'S REDEMPTION
THROUGH LIFE'S TRAUMAS

Rhonda Abellera

Trilogy Christian Publishers
A Wholly Owned Subsidiary of Trinity Broadcasting Network
2442 Michelle Drive
Tustin, CA 92780

Copyright © 2021 by Rhonda Abellera

All Scripture quotations, unless otherwise noted, taken from THE HOLY BIBLE, NEW INTERNATIONAL VERSION®, NIV® Copyright © 1973, 1978, 1984, 2011 by Biblica, Inc.® Used by permission. All rights reserved worldwide.

Scripture quotations marked (KJV) taken from *The Holy Bible, King James Version.* Cambridge Edition: 1769.

All rights reserved, including the right to reproduce this book or portions thereof in any form whatsoever.

For information, address Trilogy Christian Publishing
Rights Department, 2442 Michelle Drive, Tustin, Ca 92780.
Trilogy Christian Publishing/ TBN and colophon are trademarks of Trinity Broadcasting Network.

For information about special discounts for bulk purchases, please contact Trilogy Christian Publishing.

Manufactured in the United States of America

Trilogy Disclaimer: The views and content expressed in this book are those of the author and may not necessarily reflect the views and doctrine of Trilogy Christian Publishing or the Trinity Broadcasting Network.

10 9 8 7 6 5 4 3 2 1

Library of Congress Cataloging-in-Publication Data is available.

ISBN 978-1-64773-686-6 (Print Book)
ISBN 978-1-64773-687-3 (ebook)

With love and gratitude to Russ and Kyle, the heroes of my story and the two sons who saved my life and gave me purpose. I am forever grateful that I was privileged to raise these beautiful sons who have become such wonderful men.

CONTENTS

FOREWORD

I am thrilled to write this forward to my sister's book. I wish I could convey even more of the history of our childhood and young adult years so that you, the reader, could grasp how unexpected and horrific these storms were in our lives. Suffice it to say, our firm foundation on the Rock, Jesus, helped us weather some very un-Christian storms. However, here is where it gets interesting: God is not worried or unnerved by our seemingly crazy circumstances. Instead, He is there, holding out His arms, cradling His precious children, and infusing us with ridiculous strength and hope.

Yes, He's in the storm, seeing us through. Sometimes He whispers; other times, He yells, "She is Mine! Leave her alone!"

Sometimes, when you feel like you are His favorite, you probably are.

—Carma Hunter

ACKNOWLEDGMENTS

Writing my story seemed like a good idea at the time, but in all honesty, it became a treacherous trip down memory lane that brought up some things that my family has rarely talked about. I was determined to remember and talk about those events because in the midst of sorrow came the redeeming part of the story. It became apparent to me that it was worth sharing.

I am so grateful for the encouragement and creative input of my son, Kyle. His creativity gave me ways to share my story that I wouldn't have thought about. He encouraged me to tell my story and provided many insights from his childhood.

I am so thankful to my friend Dianna for her insight and suggestions for going deeper and telling the truth of my story.

I want to thank my sister Carma, who read several versions of the manuscript and provided her insights and edits. She helped me remember and tell some details that I had forgotten.

I also appreciate my brother Brad, who gave me some valuable insight and details that he had recalled and allowed me to share them.

I am grateful for my mother Joy, my sister Krista, my son and daughter-in-law Russ and Annie, and my daughter and son-in-law Nicole and Ben, who read an early version of my manuscript and gave me encouragement to keep writing.

I want to acknowledge my lifelong friends, Julie, Deanna, Tami, Wendy, Lori, Liz, Sandy, Tracy, Lynne, and Melissa. Even though I may not have mentioned some of you specifically, I hope you can see yourself in the pages where I talked about my tribe of friends and those who walked with me and shared my life. It was your words of encouragement, steady love, and friendship that held me together during the times I felt like I was unraveling. I hope you know how grateful I am to you for being there for me every step of the way.

To my husband Charlie, you are also the hero of my story, and I am so grateful that you entered my life when you did. You have always been a rock and have loved me and our family well. Thank you for letting me also tell your story, which became our story.

INTRODUCTION

Journal Entry—March 25, 2020

> *"Trust in the Lord with all your heart, And lean
> not unto your own understanding; In all your ways
> acknowledge Him, And He shall direct your paths"*
> *(Proverbs 3:5, NKJV).*

There is a benefit to aging. It's the ability to look back and see the timeline of your life: where you started, how far you have come, and how things have worked out, good or bad. You can see where you shouldn't have bothered to worry and times when you should have prayed harder. We don't get to see the future; we just have to live for today, full of faith and hope for tomorrow. If you can do that without regrets about your past, then you live a blessed life, but most people have some form of trauma from their past that they have to deal with. We all have gone through storms that have knocked us down or have kept us from living our best life.

As I walked along the beautiful Deschutes River that runs right through the Old Mill in Bend, Oregon, I was struck by the diversity of the river. At times, it was calm and serene. The ducks could enjoy a lazy paddle and the dogs and children could easily jump into the river and play. As I followed the path along the river, there were boulders in the middle of it with white water crashing over them. Further and further along the river, the current became stronger and faster. There was no one in the water there. Canoes and paddle boats could not manage the difficult waters over rocks, downed tree branches, and boulders.

I continued on my hike, and after climbing to the very top of the cliff and looking down, there was a breathtaking view of crashing white water plummeting over the rocks with sprays of moisture forming small rainbows in the sunlight. The river was a clear, vibrant blue and it sounded like the volume of crashing waves had been turned up. There was not a cloud in the sky as I surveyed this magnificent sight.

Looking at the river reminded me of my life. I could see times where I was thrust into the turbulent waters, trying to pull myself out of the current when the storms of life unleashed their fury. Trees and limbs that crossed over the waters were the times of deliverance. Sometimes, it came directly from the people God put in my life; other times, it was a divine, unexpected miracle.

I've had my share of storms. Some have come out of nowhere and have destroyed everything in their path. Some took time to brew, but eventually unleashed their mighty fury on everything and everyone in their way. I do know one thing for certain: I am so grateful for the choppy waters in the storm, for out of those storms and terrifying waters, I came to know the One who whispers in the storm.

As I paused to reflect and tried to remember, I was overwhelmed by rushing emotions as I thought about the past and the things that had transpired. The journals I had kept over the years helped me to remember. I felt a wave of sadness. It overwhelmed me. Those seasons felt like someone else's life.

I indulged in those memories because I am very sentimental. Those seasons of life are the ones that hold the dearest memories along with the most traumatic. If I wanted to remember those events in the past, I knew that I also needed to remember the heartache and the trauma that weaved through them. So, I paused to remember, and held my breath as the memories came flooding back.

CHAPTER ONE

When My World Fell Apart

It was a bright, sunny day in May of 1987 when my world fell apart. I had driven outside our small town up a steep mountain hilltop that overlooked the whole city of Watsonville, California, where I had grown up. As I turned into the look-out area, waves of grief and thundering sobs overwhelmed me. How could he leave me, nine months pregnant and with a small boy? What diabolical plot had consumed him and made him into someone I didn't even recognize?

I loved my children's father: a blond-haired, blue-eyed athletic and charismatic young man who had charmed me at just sixteen years of age. We married young, full of dreams and ambitions. He wanted to be a professional baseball player and I wanted to be a mother. We sang our own songs that we had written and joined a country gospel band together with another couple. I played the piano and he sang and played the bass guitar. Early in our relationship, we prayed together, went to church, and even played Mary and Joseph in our church production. Everyone that knew us thought we were the perfect couple, and in my mind, that was a recipe for a strong marriage and future.

A foreign thought hit me, one I had never had before. If I just stepped on the gas, the car would plummet to the bottom of the mountain, and my pain would be over. As I contemplated that scenario, the sobs came faster and harder. That thought went against everything I believed in, but so did the thought of my husband leaving me.

There surely must be a mistake, I thought. Yes, we had issues in our marriage, but didn't everyone? I pushed aside the nagging thoughts and memories of our fights. I usually ended up in tears, and he would storm out of the house, driving furiously down the road. I didn't really know what our fights were about, except that I seemed to ignite an anger in him

"Divorce didn't happen to people like us."

that would take days to cool. I didn't know where he would go, and my imagination would haunt me well into the night. I always prayed that he would come home. Most every night, he did. Maybe he was reeling from the disappointment of not making a career in baseball, or not being very successful with his music. I know those silent demons tormented him. He struggled to find purpose and meaning in his life, but I could not give him those.

Sometimes, it seemed that he would have a change of heart when he would come home, and he would be all smiles, hugging me as if nothing had happened, as if it were normal to disappear for hours or even overnight with no explanation. I don't know why I allowed that kind of behavior, not asking questions or demanding answers. I was just relieved to have him home again, engaging and playful with our son and being loving to me. His warm welcome would dissolve all my fears for the time being. My heart would leap, and I would look at my young son and tell him that all was well. I adopted the mindset of my mother, who said, "You just put your head down and get through it. God is enough, and you just trust in Him." I'm honestly not sure what all that meant, except to just get up every day and put one foot in front of the other. Divorce didn't happen to people like us. We were a good, solid, church-going family. I didn't even know anyone that was divorced. There wasn't anyone in my family that had been divorced, so why should this happen to me?

My mind flashed back to our wedding. He sang to me and promised to love me. We were the perfect couple. We fell in love that first summer in his 1955 Chevy truck. We were both so young and I was so impressed with him. He was so funny and charming. I would sit in the bleachers and watch him play baseball. He'd hit homeruns and I would cheer, not as loud as his mother, but I would clap my hands. His mother and I bonded on those bleachers. We had something in common: we both adored him. It was easy to fall in love with his family. His father treated me like the daughter he never had, and I was happy to fill that role. It was a jolt to my heart the first time I entered their home after we separated; all the pictures of me and of my husband were gone. It felt like a death sentence; like someone had died. Inside, I knew it was my marriage that had taken the fatal blow.

Suddenly, a hawk flew down through the trees, and the warm sunshine fell on my face through the windshield of the car. It was at that moment, then and there, that I decided to live my new life and raise my boys myself. I was strong enough and I was sure I could give them all the love they needed. It was there that I formulated my plan. I would make a happy, loving home for them, even if I had to move back into my parents' home. I didn't know how I would provide for them, but I would.

As I backed the car up onto the road, I drove down the mountain with a new sense of purpose. I patted my sweet unborn baby and told him that his mother would never leave him and that she would love him and give him and his brother a good life.

OUR OWN FAMILY UNIT

Kyle Jeffrey was born in June and his brother Russell and I welcomed him into our small little family, surrounded by a larger family of aunts, uncles, and grandparents. We made our new little home in the master bedroom of my mother and father's house. The room was large enough for a single bed on one wall and a single bed and crib on the other.

It was there that I fell in love with my newborn son Kyle. His brother and I shared a love for him that bonded us together and to him. I was still hopeful and prayed that their father and I would reconcile. However, even the birth of our son didn't soften his heart towards me. As soon as Kyle was born, my sister remembers him saying, "You had your workout, now it's time for mine," as he headed to the gym.

The disappointment seemed to loom over my head like a cloud, gradually choking out the hope, and it grew thicker with every passing week. The brokenness of my heart somehow regained some feeling and emotion as I cared for this newborn.

Having two boys to love and take care of gave me hope and purpose. They gave me a reason to get out of bed in the morning despite my shell-shocked state. Living in my mother and father's home had some advantages. I had my mother to help with the baby; I also worked in her daycare and earned a bit of income to support myself and my children. Those were precious times. I was paid by my mom to take care of my baby while watching toddlers in her daycare.

I'd watch the daycare children during the day, and then at night, I'd bring my two boys into our bedroom and tuck them in. As I tucked them in, their sweet smiles and their bright eyes focused on my face and told me that they trusted me. I was their world, and I was all they needed for now. I had to reaffirm myself daily with purpose. Yes, I could raise these boys. I could do this; God would help me, I was quite certain.

Russ was the one that kept me laughing. He was quite a trickster, and he would play with his little brother and make him laugh until his giggle sounded like that of a laughing hyena. Even at a young age, Russ took on the mantle as the man of the house. I don't know how he knew what to do, but he seemed to understand more than I could ever explain to him. He and his baby brother would go to their father's house every other weekend. For a long time, I mourned those weekends. I worried, stressed, and counted the hours until I could go pick them up and bring them home. It was during one of those weekends that I was expressing myself to the Lord:

"God, don't you know that my boys need a full-time father? How can I be everything they need?"

A lot of those weekends were very lonely for me. In desperation, I would often read through chapters of the Bible, trying to find answers. I came across a passage in Isaiah 54:13 (NIV) that said, "All your children will be taught by the Lord, and great will be your children's peace." In all my struggling and despair, that verse brought comfort to me, and I began to ask God to be the Father they needed.

"All your children will be taught by the Lord, and great will be your children's peace."
Isaiah 54:13 (NIV)

It was one of those weekends that had been especially hard, and I had both boys in the bathtub. Just six years apart, they were doing what boys do: splashing water on the floor, playing, and roughhousing in the tub. I remember praying silently that God would protect them. I worried about their lives. How would they grow up to be healthy men or fathers? It was then that I heard them bellow out a song, "For thine is the Kingdom and the power and the Glory forever, amen."[1] There they were singing—not just any song, but a song that they must have heard at church sometime that had been planted deep in their hearts. I began to believe that God had not forgotten me and knew that my boys needed Him, and so did I.

RUSS

As Russ grew into a teenage boy, I wanted to make sure I spent enough time with him. I would take him to the fair, the boardwalk, and Giants games. We were pals and really enjoyed doing things together.

When Russ was born in 1980, his dad and I had just moved into a big red farmhouse. It sat back across an apple orchard and a cow pasture. This home had five bedrooms, a huge dining room, and an old-fashioned front porch with a garden in front. I remember the sound of the screen door when it closed against the front door. It squeaked as it hit the door frame.

I remember every inch of the hardwood floor and where it met the carpet in the living room, because I cleaned and vacuumed every inch of that house. I poured my love into that home and it became a haven and refuge for my son and me. I remember decorating his nursery with the Bambi print my mother had sewed for me. I loved making sure that my son had his own room, a place where he felt loved and protected.

We had to put a floor heater in his room because our house was so cold. The fireplace downstairs barely heated the front room, and we couldn't afford to buy the propane to heat the house. I just remember the cold. Russ would shiver and cry when I dressed him and I would put layers of jammies on him until he looked like a stiff snowman. In the lonely hours of the night, as I walked the floor with him, I tried to comfort him from the horrible pangs of colic. I would sing to him Kenny Rogers love songs. "You decorated my life," I sang as I paced the floor back and forth, jiggling and rocking him until the pain subsided.[2] There, I lavished all my love on him.

During those years, Russ was a happy little boy. He was the joy and delight of our whole family: the first grandchild, the first great-grandchild, and the first nephew of my siblings. He didn't seem to realize that his father and I struggled. I would try to cushion the impatience of his father from Russ. He didn't understand the deep and buried struggles of his dad, so I tried to minimize their inter-actions. Whether right or wrong, I always tried to make everything okay.

Russ brought out the laughter in me. Even as a young boy, his wit and sense of humor brought me joy. We would take long walks together down the dirt road to look at the cows. He would point and call them "baby tows".

KYLE

When Kyle was born, a lot of people pitied me because I was a single mom with a little boy and a newborn baby, but I was so grateful for that newborn son. I always knew that Kyle was a special gift from the Lord. God knew that I would need to be loved intensely by this boy, and Kyle did love intensely, even as a young boy.

Kyle truly experienced being raised by a single mom. I went to work when he was six months old while we still lived with my mother and father. I remember trying to get out the door to get to work on time, Kyle hanging on my leg and crying for me not to go. It broke my heart and made me more determined to give Kyle a normal childhood. I would peel him away and hand him back to my mother as I jumped in the car, late for work.

All throughout my boys' grade school and high school years, they went to Christian schools. My grandparents paid for their education, which I was so grateful for. Kyle's talents began to blossom as he performed in school musicals, and in high school, he led worship in chapel and our church's youth group.

I really don't know what Kyle thought when I would take him to his dad's house every other weekend and drop him off. Many times, when he was little, he would cry because he had to go, and I would promise him a prize on his bed when he got home if he was good. When I think about those days, I am so thankful for his brother Russ. Russ was the glue that surrounded our little family. Kyle loved him dearly and always tried to be like him.

CHAPTER TWO

Joy Comes In The Morning

Journal Entry—January 1988

> *"Weeping may endure for a night, but joy comes in the morning" (Psalm 30:5, NKJV).*

My mother is a pretty tough cookie. She's a survivor. She has had to deal with more than her share of trouble. I adopted this view of her not necessarily because I first did so when I was a kid, but because of the things that happened later in her life.

She was raised by her mom: a pretty feisty and fiery preacher who moved over forty-nine times in her life. I know this because she wrote a book entitled *Forty-Nine Doors*. My grandma's husband would build churches all over the south and my grandmother would preach in them. Many times, my mother and her five siblings didn't have a home and lived in tents. I never knew my grandfather, because he died when my mother was young, but I did know "Grandma Faggie", as we called her, which was short for "Fagerstrom". She lived with us for a time when we were kids. She'd make us "baby coffee" and tell us stories about her adventures. She was a songwriter and loved the Lord passionately. Many times, early on Sunday mornings, she would wake up, sing, and play the piano, much to my father's dismay, but she also taught me how to play the piano and make homemade rolls. Although my mother is a very polished, kind, and endearing woman, she does have a side of her that reminds me of my feisty Grandma Faggie.

My mother tells stories of her brothers, three older and one younger, teasing her and harassing her as a young girl. One of them even cut her with his knife. Her sister Rose was the oldest and had married and moved out by the time my mom was born. She had to learn how to stick up for herself, and I think that's where she acquired the confidence she has. My mother didn't share in my grandmother's passion for preaching, but she preached without words. Her peaceful, quiet confidence spoke volumes to us. She also never played the piano, but said that instead, she "played her stereo".

"She preached without words."

My mom never worked outside the home and preferred to stay home and take care of her four kids. She always had a project going and was always cleaning, redecorating, or painting one of our rooms. She could turn a corner in the garage into an inviting, cozy spot, and I was usually the one who slept in the garage.

My mother was instrumental in my survival as a single mom. She modeled what being a kind, understanding mom was.

During the years I was raising my sons, my mom filled in the places that I couldn't, like cooking, doing laundry, and cleaning the house. When we lived with her, she would send me outside to play with the boys. Whether it was pitching a ball to them or playing catch, I would spend those evenings doing things that little boys liked to do. They were my life. In her wisdom, she knew that the most important thing that I could do would be to spend time with them.

"Joy comes in the morning."

I love that verse in the Bible that says, "Joy comes in the morning" (Psalms 30:5,

22

NIV). That verse has a lot of meaning to me because my mother's name is Joy, and I would always anticipate her coming in the morning to help me with my kids. As they got older, I would actually deliver them to her in the daycare when I went to work, but the point is, I needed Joy in the morning. I would soon find out in my life that I would also need joy in my mourning.

MY CHILDHOOD

I was born four weeks early and weighed just four pounds. My dad often told me he could hold me in just one hand. I adored my dad. He roughhoused with me and my sister, Carma, who is just eighteen months younger than me. He would swing us around in the backyard until we were too dizzy to stand up. We'd fall to the ground laughing, begging him to do it again. He built us our own playhouse with a window and a door and put in a small pool with a slide in the backyard.

I was a very shy and quiet girl, and I loved to stay home and ride my horse. My horse was the only friend I needed besides my sister. School was a hardship I had to endure, and it only magnified my shy, introverted personality. I lived for the day to be over so that I could go home and ride my horse.

My dad wasn't a horse person, and it really helps to be one if you have horses; otherwise, they are miserable beasts that just eat hay and poop.

For some reason, my parents agreed to let me buy a horse when I had saved up one hundred dollars (I truly think that they never expected me to earn that much money at such a young age). At age ten, after mowing lawns for my Grandpa Ben, my dad's father, and saving every penny I received from birthdays, I had enough money. My father reluctantly took me to answer an ad for a small horse. With the fifty dollars Carma had contributed, I had just enough money, and we purchased the horse. I fell in love, and we took Daisy home. We were unaware that she had been drugged, so she appeared very easy-going. However, in no time, the true colors of the horse came out. She had been a barrel racer and ran like the wind. My dad and I both didn't know any better, and I was determined to ride that horse. I jumped into the saddle and learned to hang on for dear life (a trait that I later learned was very valuable in life).

I eventually raised an Appaloosa foal, an offspring from the mare of my Aunt Sandi, my dad's sister. She was in the states teaching school while her husband finished his military career overseas. She and I bonded during those short years. I would help her on Saturdays with cleaning her house and then we would ride horses in the afternoon. Despite my dad's reluctance in expanding our horse menagerie, I kept adding to it.

My dad had a bit of a temper, and it would flare up when dealing with my crazy horse. One time, he became so aggravated that he hauled off and punched my horse in the nose. The horse, wide-eyed, shook her head and realized that she would never mess with my dad again.

My dad was also a funny man, and loved to tell true stores that were quite embellished. He would get so tickled at the punchline that he would laugh until he cried, unable to finish the story. We would all just laugh with him.

As kids, we were often embarrassed by his antics. We always seemed to have cars that gave us trouble, but my dad managed to keep them running until he ran them into the ground. I remember one particular Sunday when we were driving home from church, for some reason, as my dad drove the car onto our road, it would no longer move forward. He was so exasperated at the car that he backed it around and continued toward home by looking over his shoulder and driving the car backwards all the way down our long road. We kids were so mortified that we dived down onto the floor of the car so that our friends wouldn't see us driving backwards. I'm pretty sure my mom would have joined us if she could have gotten away with it.

In high school, my dad bought me a used 1974 Volkswagen Karmann Ghia. It was turquoise blue and the cutest car I had ever seen. If a car could give you confidence, this one did. He also bought Carma a red one when she got her license.

Carma and I attended Monte Vista Christian School in the foothills just outside our small town on the coast of California. She had a lot more friends than I did, but we seemed to sustain a good relationship with each other most of the time. She was the queen of the verbal attack, while I was much quieter and more introverted and struggled to offer a comeback very quickly. I have often thought that she should have been a lawyer. She could back you into a corner with just a few sentences, and many times, I could only resort to slugging her.

Even though we struggled to get along as kids, we would defend and take care of each other. When we were in grade school, my friend was giving us rides on the back of his bike. Soon, it was Carma's turn, and as she hopped onto the back, her foot got caught in the chain of the bike as my friend started to pedal. She yelled, and I came running. The skin on her ankle had been torn open clear to the bone and she was on the ground crying. I picked her up, bleeding and crying, and carried her all the way back home with her kicking and screaming the whole quarter of a mile. This wasn't the first time that we watched out for each other, and it certainly wouldn't be the last.

Carma has been and still is a strategic person in my life who would become one of my best friends. She would stand up for me and defend me to the end and is much better at remembering the details of my life than I am.

Brad, my one and only brother, is seven years younger than me and is one of the most creative and talented people I know. As kids, we would create elaborate stories together and come up with strategic characters and plots in our childhood play. We would have costumes and sets and would tell the other kids who they were and how they should act. Carma and I would often rope him into doing things because he was younger. Sometimes, it was playing a baby in a baby carriage, but he didn't mind at the time, he just wanted to play with us. Brad became quite a cartoonist as a child and loved everything about Disneyland. His imagination always spurred my creativity, and as adults, we ended up working together on an Easter pageant in a church production. Brad moved to China for ten years after he married Emily, a student from China who is also very smart and talented.

I am very proud of my brother. They became a very powerful team who founded the California Kids Club and the Sunshine Foundation Orphanage in China.

Krista is my baby sister, just ten years younger than me. When mom and dad said they were going to have another baby, I wasn't too sure about that, but after she was born, she became my baby. Sometimes, when my mom had been so tired that she would just put her in her crib and let her cry herself to sleep, I would sneak into the room, pick her up, and rock her to sleep. As I cared for Krista and played with her, that no doubt prepared me for the young mother that I would become. When my babies were born, I had the innate ability to know how to love and care for them. I still have that "mother bear" love for Krista and have always wanted to protect her and make sure that she is okay. She has such a tender heart and has always loved her animals like they were her own children. She has raised two wonderful girls that take all her focus and attention.

The four of us kids weren't raised in a home that was perfect, but it was loving and peaceful. We went to church every Sunday, and that church life was a major part of our lives. We would go with my parents once a month to clean the church, and often, we would play church. My siblings would take the offering and I would get up and preach, mostly because of the influence of my Grandma Hannah, my dad's mom. She would lead worship in church, and would inspire the congregation while my dad played the organ. Grandma Hannah was such a special person in my life. She would often stand me up on the church altar and make me sing while she played the piano. I would belt out old hymns, and they began to sink down into my soul. I'm pretty sure my grandmother and I shared the same heart. We spoke each other's language. She had a profound influence on my faith.

AUNT RUTHIE AND UNCLE WAYNE

Uncle Wayne was my mom's oldest brother. In his twenties and thirties, he was a traveling evangelist and would often stop and visit us when he was in town. He was the "fun uncle" that would tell you stories and give you pony-back rides on his back. He was a cowboy and would even bring his horse to visit us in our backyard.

When we were young, Uncle Wayne moved to Monterey, California and pastored a church there for many of the servicemen and women who were stationed at Fort Ord. We would often visit him in his church and he would make me and my siblings come in front and sing to the congregation. I remember going up the stairs into the back of the church to a large room where they would gather after service for a potluck. It's funny, the things you remember as a kid; I would

"I didn't need to ask anyone who that was in the picture, I knew that the one guiding the man in the storm was Jesus."

often stare at the large painting of a man with his hands on the steering wheel of a ship in the midst of a storm, trying to see through the rain. Behind him stood a man pointing in a direction to guide him through the storm. I didn't need to ask anyone who that was in the picture; I knew that the one guiding the man in the storm was Jesus. I have thought about that picture many times during my life, as I have often felt like that man in the boat in the middle of the storm with Jesus pointing the way.

Uncle Wayne's life dramatically changed when he met Ruth Bosak, and so did ours. She had a bigger-than-life personality and a laugh that would engage the whole room. Her blonde, Dolly Parton-styled wigs along with bright blue eyeshadow and pink lips were her signature look, and she wore them proudly with the sass and spunk of a Hollywood movie star.

When Uncle Wayne brought her to our home to meet us, we were at first a bit shocked. She was twenty years his junior, and we wondered if Uncle Wayne knew what he was getting into. It turns out he did: he was smitten, and we were delighted. She seemed shy at first, but instantly, she fell in love with us kids, especially my brother. She stayed in the family room, reading books to us the whole time while Uncle Wayne visited with my mom and dad. From that moment, we developed a bond with Aunt Ruthie that lasted our entire lifetime. She was the "fun aunt" that loved shopping, going out to eat, Disneyland, and the dinner theater. She and Uncle Wayne lived in southern California after they married, and we visited them every Thanksgiving and always went to Disneyland. It became a long-standing tradition in our family, and after I had my boys, I continued on with that tradition. They would come to our house for Christmas, and we called her "Mrs. Claus" because she would bring a trunk-load of presents. No one could keep up with Aunt Ruthie.

Uncle Wayne pastored a small home-missionary church, and even as a child, I could understand his messages and I loved listening to his booming preaching voice. Aunt Ruthie was a schoolteacher and was the kind of teacher that loved her children and was adored by them.

When my dad passed away, my mom became Aunt Ruthie's traveling buddy. Uncle Wayne was too fragile to travel much anymore, so together, they went on trips to Hawaii and went on cruises to the Caribbean, Bahamas, Mexico, and Alaska.

AUNT RUTHIE

Journal Entry—December 2, 2015

I am in Southern California in Ruthie's house with my mom. I am making funeral arrangements and calling lawyers, appraisers, and locksmiths. It seems so surreal.

It was in 2015 that my mom and I decided to fly down to Chino, California to visit with my Aunt Ruthie for Thanksgiving. She had been in and out of the hospital and really needed our help. Uncle Wayne had passed away a few years before, and we felt like Aunt Ruthie was really reaching out to us.

My mom and I met at the Orange County Airport and made our way to the hospital. We had planned all kinds of activities to do with my aunt, hoping she would be released from the hospital that week.

However, upon our arrival, we found out she was much sicker then we realized. She had just been diagnosed with cancer. She had all kinds of medical issues and was determined to get out of the hospital when we were there. My mother and I ended up staying in her home for most of the week, trying to help my aunt with details.

Aunt Ruthie called me over to her bedside in the hospital and whispered in my ear some things she wanted me to do for her. During that week, I paid her bills, put my name on her bank accounts, and went out and picked up pizza for her. Little did I know that it would be her last meal.

I did anything she asked. I wasn't always the one closest to Aunt Ruthie, but during the last few years, whenever I would see her, she would tell me how wonderful my boys were and what a good job I had done. That meant the world to me; I so wanted her to be proud of me.

My aunt had assigned me as executor of her estate, and I had no idea what that meant, but I would find out very shortly.

I flew back home the Friday after that Thanksgiving, knowing that I'd never see my Aunt Ruthie alive again. I called my cousin Darla in Texas, who was also very close to her, and said, "If you want to see Aunt Ruthie alive, you'd better leave now!" Darla had spent many summers along with her high school years in our home, and had often accompanied us on our trips to Aunt Ruthie's house. I knew that she had a unique relationship with Aunt Ruthie and had promised her that she'd be there when she passed. Darla kept that promise and arrived at the hospital just in time to hold Aunt Ruthie's hand as she slipped into eternity on December 1, 2015.

From there, my life changed; I had no idea what was about to happen that year.

Because it was so close to Christmas, we had a small gathering at the graveside in December, and I planned to have a larger memorial service for Ruthie in January. I knew that her friends, family, and fellow teachers would want an opportunity to honor her.

I was honored to be the executor of my aunt's estate. The next year, I was flying down to Chino, California at least once a month. There, I hired a professional estate sale lady who literally saved my life. She and her team went through the whole house, throwing out the junk and organizing the treasures. I had taxes to file, repairs on the home to oversee, tons of files and paperwork to go through, and money to distribute.

My Aunt Ruthie was a "high-end hoarder", as Carma called her. She loved shopping and was an extremely generous gift-giver. Her many friends, students, and coworkers showered her with gifts as well. Over the years, Ruthie's house became filled with all these wonderful treasures until you literally had no room to even walk through the house.

It took a whole team, and I am so grateful for Aunt Ruthie's friends, who helped me because of their deep love for their friend Ruthie and who directed me to the proper professionals. As always, Carma was there to help me with the estate sale, and after one whole year, everything had been sold and distributed.

CHAPTER THREE

─••─────•─────••─

Returning To My Roots

Journal Entry—January 1988

I am determined to find a job. I've got to provide for my boys somehow.

W hen you go through a trauma in your life, especially a divorce, you struggle with anger and unforgiveness. You wonder what you did wrong and what you did to deserve this catastrophic event in your life. I did. I didn't realize that it affected me in every way, but the anger served as a catalyst to spring me into action. As a young, thirty-year-old divorced woman, I didn't want to babysit in my mother's daycare the rest of my life, so I worked on my resume and was determined to find a job.

My resume was very sparse; I had only worked in the church office a short time before I became pregnant. The only other job experience I had was giving piano lessons, and that didn't present very well on a resume. However, I was determined to make a way for my boys. I took on the mantle of being their sole provider, and I took that role very seriously.

I also wanted to get back into church. The ordeal of getting divorced and having a new baby was overwhelming for me, and I found it very difficult as a single mother to attend church by myself. The label I wore on my forehead screamed "divorced"! In the eighties, there wasn't much emphasis on counseling or mentoring, but I was determined to forge a new life for myself. I returned to the small church that I had grown up in. My family had long since moved to a new up-and-coming church where I had been going, but I didn't feel like I could face anyone there.

"The label I wore on my forehead screamed divorced!"

It was a new world for me, being divorced, raising my sons, and figuring out how to survive in a world that I could not control; a world that had swept away dreams that I had for my life. Now, instead of living my dreams, I just wanted to survive each day.

The Lord sent me some special friends, David and Lois King, who had moved to Watsonville to pastor the church of my childhood. There, I would begin to heal, slowly learning how to trust again. Lois, the longtime childhood friend of my mother, embraced this broken single mom and began to breathe some life back into her bones. My friend Sandy Grazian also took me under her wing and loved me unconditionally.

As I think back now, I was probably like a drowning victim tied around their necks. However, in spite of me hanging on to them for dear life, they seemed to accept the assignment. These women who modeled the kind of loving mother that I wanted to be became the glue that helped put me back together.

These friends were gifts to me; they loved unconditionally and tolerated all the facets of my despair. They loved me without judgement and taught me how to love people that way. I didn't realize it at the time, but in conjunction with my healing, I was being mentored for future ministry. So many times, I have caught myself saying the same things they said to me. They weren't afraid to dive deep with me into my pain; to get their hands dirty. I was able to unload my broken heart into their hands, and slowly, I felt new life returning to me.

A NEW LIFE

Even though I was far from being whole, I knew that God had something more for me. I began to feel restless and was anxious to get more involved in a church. I returned to my former church, Green Valley, where I would begin to build a new life. It took more courage than I can begin to describe to attend a bigger church where I still wore the label of "divorced".

New pastors, Dennis and Deanna Smith, had just come to Green Valley Church in 1990, and I felt like this is where I wanted to raise my boys. Deanna, who was the music pastor, started a new choir. I loved to sing, and some of my greatest memories were from high school, where I joined the traveling choir as an eighth-grader. I was one of two eighth-graders who got to travel because we both played the clarinet. Those years that I traveled with the school choir, singing in many churches, shaped my heart for ministry. Dan Stump, our choir director, fueled my desire to sing and minister because of his heart for God and for people.

After joining the Green Valley choir, I began to finally make some new friends. Little did I know that these new friends would form a tribe of women who would stick with me through many of the traumas I would face. In the years to come, I would need them, and they would be there. They all homeschooled their children, and as desperately as I wanted to be a part of that club, I had to get out and find a job.

I'm amazed at how God places the people you need in your life at the time you need them. Dianna Salciccioli was a childhood friend who moved back to Watsonville to serve at Green Valley Church with her husband, Greg. She also was the kind of friend that I would call a "stretcher friend"; she was not afraid to go deep with you and walk with you through your trauma. I find it interesting that during those years, I didn't reach out to a counselor, even though I really needed it. I just couldn't find a way to let go of my deep pain. However, the friends in my life became my life counselors, and sometimes, that is all you need: someone to love you and walk through life with you.

FINDING A JOB

Dianna, knowing my plight as a single mom, mentioned to her father that I needed a job. He owned an engineering company and hired me on the spot. I was stunned. I barely knew my way around the office. An older lady who worked there also went to our church and was in charge of training me. She was so kind and patient. She literally had to show me how to turn on a computer. If it hadn't been for her, I never would have learned all the basics that I needed for my next job. She also would encourage me in the Lord, and her wisdom and compassion fed my worn-out soul. Sometimes, you don't realize that some things in life are a preparation for the next step in your journey. Looking back, I could see that God was preparing me for my future.

That position lasted one year, and I was again looking for a job. My friend Sandy told me that her husband heard about my situation and was willing to ask his friend at his company about an open position. He worked for Granite Construction, a local company in town, and thought they might need a receptionist. I interviewed for the job and was hired on the spot. I don't even know why they hired me, but little did I know that for the next twenty years, God would use this company to provide a job for me, provide medical insurance for my boys, and even throw in a few Giants tickets along the way.

I poured myself into my job, and God once again put people in my life that I needed. I worked in three different departments throughout my career and was blessed to have made some wonderful friends, but being single in a male-dominated company was something I was not prepared for. I learned some quick lessons on how to manage myself, and as a young single mom, I felt very vulnerable, like I needed a husband, a protector in my life.

My boys were getting older; they were involved in school and they were thriving. I was still living in one of my Grampa Ben's rentals; I loved living there on my own, out of my parents' home, and began to think about dating.

I had been divorced a couple of years, and my ex-husband had already remarried. I soon joined the dating scene, but it proved to be heartbreaking. My dates became one counseling session after another, trying to console the men who were also divorced and "looking for love". Because of my brokenness and trust issues, I had such high standards for men that no one survived more than three months with me. I continued this cycle for many years, and finally concluded that when you are looking to fill the holes in your life with another person who is also broken, you will end up empty. I continued to fill up the emptiness with my boys, but even their love couldn't heal me completely.

> *"When you are looking to fill the holes in your life with another person who is also broken, you will end up empty."*

I began to throw myself into various groups in my church. This was a thriving community of wonderful friends. We all sang in the choir together and became a close-knit family. My boys were embraced by this community, and often my friend's husband would take them on camping trips and include them in many activities. They grew up in the church, barely feeling the sting of not living with their dad. There were many dads who embraced them and took an interest in them.

When Pastor Dennis asked me to teach a single-moms class, it was there that I began to feel like I had something to give. I would prepare messages for that class, but in reality, the class was for me; I was preaching to myself.

The day that Deanna called me at work and asked me to help her with the Christmas production was the day I made a pivotal decision that would not only help give me purpose, but would give opportunities for my boys to participate in something bigger than themselves. They both played their instruments in the orchestra and fine-tuned their musical abilities under the direction of our music director. Other times, they would join the backstage crew or help with the construction of sets and backdrops. We were dearly loved by these friends, and we grew closer as a little family within the larger family in our church.

What I didn't realize at the time was that for the next twenty-five years, Deanna and I would work together on countless productions and ministry trips and would build our friendship on our love of ministry and the Lord. That love forged a bond of sisterhood that would take us through many trials and experiences that would sometimes try our friendship, but bind us together in an unshakable bond.

The ministry at Green Valley was my calling, and I felt like I could finally remove the "divorce" label that I had been carrying around. Because of the love of so many friends, I no longer felt like a misfit. My tribe of friends were the angels that God gave to me. I had found a home that carried me through many storms to come.

CHAPTER FOUR

The Earthquake

I find it strange that the natural disasters that take place in our lives often parallel personal traumas that occur (or maybe that's just me). 1989 was a year of upheaval and trauma in my family's lives. Carma had been dating Ken Hunter from Eugene and they were engaged to be married in the summer. I was very happy for her, but at the same time, it was traumatic for me. Emotionally, I felt like I was in no shape to stand up as co-maid of honor with her best friend. I felt emotionally ragged and wondered how I would get on with my life when I still felt so broken. I was able to hold back the tears and smile during the wedding, but it left me devastated at my own circumstances. It had only been two years since my husband had left me.

I had just moved into one of my Grandpa Ben's rentals and created a cozy home for my boys when a devastating event occurred that shook our family to the core: I began to notice something odd about my dad. I approached friends and family about his strange behavior. It wasn't anything I could really put my finger on, but there were long stretches in his day that he couldn't account for. He was distant and quiet. His usual joking around with the family was nonexistent.

I was more suspicious than my mom or my siblings, and as my suspicions grew, we, along with our pastors, confronted him as a family. Finally, after hours of direct confrontation, he admitted to having an affair. My mother was heartbroken and shocked. "Things are going to change around here," she said. She demanded that he end his affair if he wanted to live in her house and stay married. He sheepishly said that he would and that he wanted to restore his marriage. I often wondered how he felt, being confronted by his pastor and his family. How could you ever get over the shame of that? She took him back, but I don't think things were ever the same again; they sure weren't for me or my siblings. Once this card had been played, it was impossible to take it back. My father had created a seed of distrust in us, and I wrestled with this for the years to come.

"I find it strange that the natural disasters that take place in our lives often parallel personal traumas that occur."

In those years, my dad was kind and considerate to my mom, and they seemed to have made amends. It wasn't a real, loving relationship, but it was somewhat peaceful. However, as much as I loved my dad, it was over for me. The image of the dad I knew and loved was forever shattered, especially when I had relied on him to be there for me and my boys. I wondered if things could ever be normal again.

Little did we know that this event in our lives was a precursor to another tragic event that year. On one hot October afternoon, I was giving piano lessons in my home to an older woman. My boys were at my mom's daycare. As I looked out the window, I saw my car in the driveway starting to hop up and down. My little house began to shake as if someone were shaking a cereal box. The lady I was teaching screamed, and I yelled, "Get in the doorway!" The great 6.9 Loma Prieta Earthquake hit the San Francisco Bay Area and shook us to our core. The earthquake was centered near Loma Prieta Peak in the Santa Cruz Mountains, just thirty minutes north of Watsonville. It devastated many buildings in our town and caused the collapse of the San Francisco-Oakland Bay Bridge. That quake seemed to physically demonstrate the quake I felt inside. Nothing seemed like it would ever be the same again.

When the house stopped shaking, the piano lesson was definitely over, and I jumped into my car and headed to my mom's house.

I could just visualize cupboards, furniture and glass shattering in the daycare room, where most likely my boys and all the other children were. As I passed by the neighborhoods with collapsed chimneys and porches, with people pouring out into the streets, I caught myself just saying the name of Jesus over and over.

As I pulled up to the house, there on the front lawn were all the children, my boys, my mom, and her helper, Ellen, waving at me. "We're all here, we're all okay," she said. I ran over to my boys, hugging them. My mother was shaken and stunned. My mother told me that a few minutes before the earthquake, Ellen had walked over to the steps in the room, and all the children had followed her. The steps led up to the hallway, which was the safest place in the house during an earthquake. There she sat down around the children as the earthquake began to shake and all the cupboards in the room came crashing down on the cots below where the children had previously been sleeping. No one was harmed. As I walked through the house, it was in shambles. The grandfather clock had fallen and shattered, and dishes were broken all over the floor. Surely the angels had come and protected all the children and my mother. We did not realize it at the time, but God's hand was on my mother and her daycare.

The boys and I stayed with my parents for a week before moving back to our house. I was afraid to be alone at night with all the aftershocks that were occurring. My boys somehow thought it was fun to sleep out in the living room all together and cook breakfast over the barbecue. I am grateful that they seemed to have such a carefree childhood. In fact, that is pretty much how they approached most things as young boys. Everything seemed to be an adventure.

More emotional aftershocks occurred when David and Lois left the small church that I had been attending. They had been such a rock for me dealing with my father. I felt abandoned again. I didn't blame them, but I felt like another part of me had been torn away. My sister, newly married, had moved to Eugene, and now my anchors, my pastors, had moved away. The abandonment issue kept surfacing and once more raised its ugly head.

CHAPTER FIVE

The Arrest

Journal Entry—May 15, 1997

The most terrible day of my life: my dad just got arrested.

Whenever trauma strikes, it seems to happen in a split second. Everything can seem so normal, and then suddenly, out of nowhere, it can pounce on you like a lion hiding in the bush, and then it affects everything and everyone around you. It can completely pull apart your whole world.

In 1997, I had been with Granite Construction for eight years and was moving up in my career. I worked in the Media and Investor Relations department and got to go on some business trips to New York and Chicago with my boss. During this time, I found a cute Victorian house that I moved into with my boys and I began to feel like I had purpose in life. I had pretty much stopped dating, wanting to focus on my boys and my career, along with the ministry I was involved in.

Russ was a sophomore and attended Monte Vista Christian School and Kyle was ten years old, still attending Green Valley School. Even though we no longer lived in my parents' home, I was thrilled that they had my dad, who was a father figure to them. My dad was good to my boys. He took Russ golfing with him and let him help with chores around the house. Many times, I would come home from work and Russ would be climbing around on the roof, right behind my father, fixing a leak or cleaning out the gutters. He took the boys to their baseball practices and always seemed willing to pitch a ball to them.

My dad never really had a solid career. He struggled as a real estate agent and had a few good years in working for his father, but he was never very successful. My dad tried construction and various other jobs, but as he aged, he never seemed to be satisfied. When my sister and her husband Ken moved back to Watsonville, he and my dad managed a hitch shop together, selling and installing hitches on cars and trucks. My dad seemed to sabotage every opportunity he had. I couldn't really understand that, because he was so smart and charismatic. Eventually, he seemed satisfied to just help my mom with her daycare. They would shop for groceries every Saturday and he would help watch children during the week. Oftentimes, he would pick kids up from school and bring them to the daycare. He also took my boys to school and picked them up, and because I worked, I was so grateful for the help.

However, the thread of doubt and distrust for him would always surface. I could never quite put my finger on it, but the feelings about him became stronger and stronger. He had changed, and I didn't know exactly how or when. I would watch him, and what used to bring him joy and happiness didn't seem to anymore. I can only describe the way his eyes were. They no longer sparkled when he talked, and he didn't laugh like he used to laugh. Gone were the funny stories; instead, there were just blank stares. He and my mom used to be best friends, and throughout my childhood, they seemed to really enjoy each other, but now, there seemed to be tension once again between them. I think she was feeling very frustrated with him being around the house. She was a worker and a doer, and she expected as much from him. Most afternoons, he could be found asleep on the living room couch while my mother ran to and fro working her daycare.

I was at work one typical day in May, and was surprised to hear that my best friend, Deanna, was in the lobby waiting to see me. When I saw her, I knew something was terribly wrong.

"Is there someplace where we can go to talk?" She asked.

I showed her into an office and sat down.

"Your father has been arrested, and I wanted to come and tell you in person." I felt frozen, glued to my seat. I tried to digest what she had just said, not realizing that our lives would be forever changed by that one sentence.

Deanna and Dennis, as our close friends and pastors, had apparently been warned by the sheriff of my father's arrest.

Although I no longer lived with my parents, my boys went there every day after school. I remember just a few weeks earlier walking from the side patio into the large daycare room one day, and a horrifying thought hit me. At that moment, I knew that somehow God had already revealed to me what had been happening in this daycare. I remember thinking, *What should I do? Is this really true, or is it just a feeling or a fleeting thought?* It made sense, however; just a few years earlier, he had kept his secret life and had deceived us all. Perhaps I should have done something; I may have been able to stop him, but I realized that I could never have controlled him; it was too big, too horrendous for any of us to manage. I began to put the pieces together and realized that God had intervened.

"I put the pieces together and realized that God had intervened."

I left my office and jumped into my car. Once again, I was experiencing another trauma; another time in my life where I had to jump into the saddle and hang on for dear life.

When I walked in the door, there were no children; no toddlers running around, no crying babies in the other room, just my mother and sister Carma sitting on the couch, sobbing. My mother just kept saying, "When the sheriff came to pick him up, he didn't even deny it."

As my mother began to recount to me what had occurred, she began to cry again with fresh waves of tears and horror. "The children, those poor children. What will happen to them? How will this affect their lives? He has not only destroyed our lives, but he has destroyed theirs as well."

A new horror filled my heart. My boys, what about my boys? What had they seen, what had they witnessed? Were they victims?

I knew that Russ was still at baseball practice, so I looked for Kyle and realized that he was outside on the patio, looking through the window. He later told me that he had watched the sheriff hand-cuff his grandpa. He had witnessed the horrible sight of my mother hugging my father goodbye with tears streaming down her face. I shudder as I picture my son watching this drama unfold. Little did we know that the only times he would ever see his grandpa again would be through the glass of a prison visiting room.

As my mother regained her composure, she looked at my sister and I and said with a shaky voice, "I don't know how we'll get through this, but we will. We have to, we have no choice. We still have our family, and, well, the rest is up to God."

I have no memory of what happened next, except that we were ashamed and devastated. For the next two weeks, my father's picture appeared all over the news. Reporters were camped outside of our home. I became the family spokesperson and tried to answer their questions as authentically as I could. I had to make statements to the press that were quoted on the air. I tried to express how heartbroken we were for the families and how devastated we were as a family. The reporters were also talking about my mother. Surely they would not implicate her? We had to get my mother out of there. We took her to San Jose, where Brad and Emily lived before their move to China, and tucked her away, hidden from the outside world.

I knew that I should stay with my mom in her home, but in the past year, I had fallen in love with the cute little Victorian house my boys and I lived in. It felt good to gain some independence, and there was nothing in me that wanted to live in my father's home again. I just couldn't do it, no matter how much my mother needed me.

However, much to my disappointment, I found out that my home had been sold, and I had to move out. My dear friend Wendy offered to let me stay in a rustic cottage that looked like a cabin, owned by her family, rent-free. That was just what I needed, and I packed up the boys and moved to the outskirts of town for a couple of months, trying to keep our lives as normal as possible.

I was honest with my boys and told them the truth, but there are things that you never expect to say to your children. Russ was a teenager, and it impacted him the most. He was so shaken up that he slept on the floor in my room, along with his brother. I clung to my little family, trying to stay afloat, but every day brought a new wave of emotion and details that nearly drowned us all.

As the story unfolded, we learned more about the treacherous details. My father had been molesting some of the young girls in the daycare. My mother had no knowledge of this atrocity going on, and was overwhelmed with a dreadful fear that she would be incriminated in this horrifying crime. It was at this time that I once again realized the protection of the hand of the Lord over her life and our family. She was not even a suspect and was declared innocent, even by the reporters on the news. We found out later that many of the mothers were heartbroken over losing my mother to care for their children. She had become a part of the family, and no one wanted to blame her.

"There are things that you never expect to say to your children."

Detectives had been following my dad around for months as they put their case together. Now, he was booked in the county jail, awaiting his trial. He pleaded no contest, not wanting to put his family through the devastation of a trial. I really believe he was relieved to get caught. I think he wanted this nightmare that he had created to be over. He was caught in the grips of something that would never let go and would eventually take his life.

I took a week off work, and when I went back, I felt the stares of everyone in my building. I could just imagine what they were saying behind my back, as if I, too, were to blame. I felt my boss turn on me, and he began to question everything I did. He began to shut me out, causing me to fear for my job. Miraculously, another manager in a different department suddenly told me that the next day, I'd be working for him. My job was rescued, but for the second time in my life, I again had a label across my forehead; I was marked. This time, the label was more shameful then the first one. I thought I'd be carrying that around for the rest of my life.

During those first few weeks, people from the church and friends all over the place called, left voicemails, and reached out to my family. It was their words of comfort and prayer that kept us going. It was our tribe of friends who came to our rescue. Carma and I were going to quit the choir and stay away from church. We could not imagine standing up in front of the congregation. By that first Sunday, everyone knew. Deanna insisted that Carma and I sing in the choir, and we did. I opened up to everyone at choir practice and told them what had happened. The offering of love from our friends and church family poured over our souls. I know that is how we survived.

I didn't visit my dad in jail, but my sister Krista did. Being the baby of the family, she had a closer relationship with my father at that time, and her innocent heart was sympathetic to her dad. I am glad he had her, because none of the rest of us could even look at him. My Aunt Carol (my dad's youngest sister) and Uncle Jim went to his sentencing and visited him many times while he was in prison. Uncle Jim talked with my dad and counseled him. I think those touches from family saved my father's life.

I didn't know what to think or how to feel, and it took me a long time to want to see him. I was still struggling with being abandoned by my husband, and now my father had not only abandoned me, but my boys were left once again without a father figure in their lives.

After his sentencing, my dad went to San Quentin State Prison, north of San Francisco for a few months. He was beat up pretty badly there; I guess that's what they do to child molesters. I could not even say the words. I couldn't comprehend what was happening. Krista was terrorized when she saw him. He was pretty shaken up, and Krista, in her true style, showed him love and compassion. I know that meant a lot to him. I still couldn't face him, and neither could my mother. I was so angry, I am ashamed to admit, that I was *glad* he got beat up, except I would have preferred to do the punching myself.

My brother Brad was grieving quite heavily for our dad. He somehow wanted to fix him. In an email to me recently, he shared his journey:

"I suppose I am heavily influenced by the hippie generation—where boys and men are encouraged to be honest about their thoughts and feelings. Any man born before WWII was simply trained to be strong, do their job, and 'suck it up' if they felt like crying. This was certainly my dad's generation, and I suppose it was a little unfair of me to impose a radically different sensibility of how men deal with their inner life.

But what was really unfair of me was to take on the role of a psychotherapist for my dad and expect him to cooperate. Indeed, I really thought I was getting somewhere when I got him to tell me, 'It all started with pornography—something I was first exposed to when I was serving in the Reserves.' I still felt like I was only scratching the surface, and my own pain was unrelenting.

In the quiet of my prayer time, I cried out to the Lord, and it was almost as if Jesus came to sit down and have coffee with me—the conversation between me and God was so real it was palpable. After His first sip of coffee, Jesus set His cup down and leaned forward, looking right into my face. 'Stop trying to fix your dad. That's My job.'

'Then what am I supposed to do?' I replied.

'Trust Me.'

'Then every conversation is just small talk? All our interaction is just surface level? He's got very deep issues he's not facing at all!'

Jesus relaxed. 'Brad, I want you to do only three things.'

I bowed my head. 'Okay, Lord. What is it?'

'Receive his phone calls, reply to his letters, and go see him when you can. And if all your conversation is small talk, I'm okay with that.'

I looked up at Him again. 'Really? That's it?'

A subtle, 'Mona Lisa' smile came over Jesus' face. 'I don't need you to do anything more.'"

As a family, we mourned for the life we once knew. We mourned for the loss of a father and grandfather, and we mourned for the lives of the children that would be changed forever. My mother had lost her daycare, her job, her home, and her dignity.

I finally went to visit my father after he was sent to Mule Creek Prison in Ione, California. After all the months of scandalous news and his sentencing, I took my mother for the first time to see him.

> *"I prayed that God would forgive him, and forgive me for the feelings I had for my father."*

We waited for him inside the visiting room after we had been screened, patted down and led into the stark, ugly room. The door opened, and in came my father, dressed in denim prison wear. His glasses were broken and taped together and his hair was longer than I had ever seen it. It's funny, the things that you notice just to distract yourself from pain. My dad greeted us warmly and my mother allowed him to hug her. I'm not ordinarily a superficial person, but I faked a smile and offered him a quick hug. I could barely look at him as he talked, sharing about his new life in prison. I hadn't yet found my way to forgiveness, but my mother was more gracious, or perhaps better at pretending.

As we left, I promised to write and to answer his phone calls, but my heart had not yet caught up. I still felt a smoldering of hate and bitterness stirring in my heart, a churning that would take many more years to contend with. I was so relieved that he was in prison, paying for his sins. I prayed that God would forgive him and forgive me for the feelings I had for my father.

CHAPTER SIX

Picking Up The Pieces

Journal Entry—August 1, 1997

> *"Then they cried out to the Lord in their trouble and He brought them out of their distress. He stilled the storm to a whisper; the waves of the sea were hushed. They were glad when it grew calm, and He guided them to their desired haven" (Psalm 107:28, NIV).*

After the dust had settled, I began to make plans to move back to my parents' home. My mother needed my financial help, and she started selling things in the home to make the mortgage payments. Krista had just gotten engaged to Bob Ross, who had been so instrumental in helping her through the trauma. He had stayed in the home on the sofa when the reporters were camping out in the front yard. Bob is an avid hunter and procurer of guns, so Krista and my mom felt safe in his capable hands. He helped Krista recover and look forward to her wedding and her new life. My mom was still left stunned and numb, wondering how she would survive.

When Krista moved out of my parents' home and into the house that she would share with her new husband, the boys and I once again moved back into "the bedroom". Here we were again. I felt like it was a huge step backwards, and I didn't know how to console my mom. I didn't know how to repair our lives, let alone hers.

Russ seemed distant. This was his final year of high school, and he was playing baseball for Monte Vista. Russ was quite a good pitcher; his father was very proud of him and loved cheering for him at his games.

So many times, I'd leave work early in hopes of getting to Russ' game. There, I'd find his dad, with Russ' stepmom and his dad's parents sitting on the bleachers, cheering for him. I would climb up to another section of the bleachers by myself, looking on at that happy couple. I wondered if, through his cheering and laughter, he was trying to show me how blessed he was in his new life. I had never felt so alone, not even in the darkness of the night, not even sitting alone in church. Baseball was for families, at least in my mind. I was not a family, sitting alone in the bleachers. He seemed to have everything he wanted. Why did he have to destroy my life to find happiness in his?

"Why did he have to destroy my life to find happiness in his?"

During those years, I knew that Russ missed his dad. He would see him every other weekend, but they never really had any alone time. As I walked over to congratulate Russ on his pitching, he moved over toward his dad. I began to feel invisible. Where had I gone wrong? Kyle was still very close to me, but I felt Russ' coolness and distance. I finally learned that Russ was dating a girl whom I had never met. I was concerned about her because she did not go to church, and I could tell that she was pulling Russ away from church and the youth group.

As a mom, I pulled out all the stops. I was diligent to learn all I could about her and her relationship with my son. The next year was painful. Russ was quiet and distant, and after he graduated high school, I felt like I was losing my son.

It was then that my mom put her house on the market and we looked for a house to move into. Russ wanted us to move to Aptos, by the beach, and my mom was anxious to get out of Watsonville.

She was working as a caregiver in Santa Cruz, and this would be an easier commute for her at night.

We found a run-down beach house down by the flats at Rio Del Mar. It was close to the beach, and I loved to run on the path along the ocean with my friends. There were four bedrooms for me, my mom, and my two boys. There, we made our new home, eager to get on with our lives.

I worried so much about Russ; he had been showing signs of partying when hanging out with guys from his team. Deanna offered to fast and pray with me, and I started a journey of prayer and believed that God would get a hold of his heart. I knew both of my boys had accepted Jesus, but I realized that sometimes, they would go through times of testing their faith and even wondering about God.

It was one night in particular that both Russ and Kyle had gone to a youth group meeting in Salinas. That youth group was having special services and had invited our youth group to participate. I was up late waiting for the boys to come home, wondering how their evening had gone. When Russ walked in the door, I looked into his eyes and there was something different about him. I hugged both of them goodnight, but I didn't know what had happened until the next morning. As I looked into the face of my oldest boy, I knew that something had changed. He explained that there had been a drama about heaven and hell. It shook him up so much that he had rededicated his life to the Lord. I was beyond thrilled. As the weeks passed by, I knew that what Russ had experienced was real, because I saw some changes in his life. However, he was facing a real dilemma: what to do about his girlfriend who did not know the Lord and did not want to go to church. I never pushed Russ to decide, because I knew that it was now his own journey, but I kept praying. I promised Russ that if he would completely surrender his life to the Lord and be obedient to Him, God would do something amazing in his life.

Russ broke up with his girlfriend after two months, and I was happy to have both my boys serving along with me at church. They both played in the orchestra, led worship in their youth group, and agreed to be a part of the stage crew in our productions. My life seemed blessed and full, but there was still something missing. As

I earnestly prayed, I began to give up on the idea of getting married again. It didn't seem like God was bringing anyone into my life; either that, or I had already scared them away.

CHAPTER SEVEN

──••▪▪━━━━━━▪━━━━━━▪▪••──

A New Life

Journal Entry—March 19, 2000

I'm so overwhelmed at God's love and provision for my life. He forgives, guides, and teaches me.

I pictured myself walking hand in hand with Jesus along the sandy beach. He carefully guided me over rocks and driftwood. We walked along, laughing and talking. He peered deep into my eyes, knowing what I'm about, knowing everything about me, yet patiently listened to me talk.

My heart leapt when He smiled at my words and encouraged my heart, but then, we stopped, and He turned toward the ocean. He began to pull me toward the water's edge. I playfully walked into the shallow water and then ran back toward the dry sand, but He grabbed my hand and began to walk again into the water. I stopped and looked deep into His eyes. I only saw peace and surrender, and His eyes compelled me to keep walking, but He knew my questions before I asked them, and He said to me,

"You must walk with me into the deeper water where the waves crash over the sand, for it's in the storms of life that you can only know the depth of

My love and the wealth of My provision. Walk into the depths of My love, dive deeply into My presence, and you will know Me in the certainty of My love."

CHARLIE

I met Charlie when he joined the choir at Green Valley. He was sometimes quiet, but also pretty outgoing and full of mischief. I normally sat in the front seats at practice, and he sat in the back and sang bass. His laughter and joking often disrupted the practice, but our music director Deanna laughed along with him. I think she loved him way before I did.

I began to work with Charlie during one of our Christmas productions. I was directing the drama and he was trying to make an angel fly. This was the first time we were performing at the performing arts center downtown, and I was thrilled to be working with professional lights, a stage, and curtains. However, we had a big predicament: in order to make our manger scene look realistic, we needed our real, live angel to fly up into the top of the rafters.

Charlie, who loves a challenge, took it on. It was pretty rough at first. How do you make a real, live person fly through the air without making them look like an acrobat in a circus? Charlie did it, and everyone started calling her "Charlie's angel".

That was just the beginning of my relationship with Charlie. I was still shy about any relationships, and I guarded my heart and the hearts of my sons. I was afraid of making another mistake, and so I treaded lightly when it came to dating. At this point, I wasn't very successful in relationships. I either frightened them away with my unreal expectations or broke their hearts before things got too serious (on my part, at least).

I noticed Charlie's tenacity and his ability to work hard when we remodeled our church. Charlie would work a forty-hour week, pick up his daughter from school, spend a couple hours with her, drop her off at her mothers', and then come to the church and work until 10:00pm. He was an electrician and did this for about a year. I also watched him stand up on the church platform when we would send out our mission teams around the world. He went everywhere. If there was a project or a trip, Charlie was all in.

Our relationship continued as friends for several years. Everyone knew Charlie. He teased all the kids and joked around with his friends from church. They were mostly older men, and he loved hanging out with them. I didn't realize at the time, but Charlie never really had a father that cared about him. His father left when he was small, and he was raised by his mother, who had many children already.

Charlie was raised, as he calls it, in the "projects" in Watsonville. We were in the same grade, but we never met until we attended church together. His mother and seven children depended on food stamps and welfare to survive. Charlie was determined to never rely on the government and went to work as a young teenager in the lettuce fields with his uncles. He later worked at the local bowling alley for several years. He wanted to buy school clothes and do things for himself.

When he split up with his wife of five years, he was devastated. Charlie tells me the story of watching his wife drive away with another man while he stood by the side of the road, holding the hand of his two-year-old daughter, Nicole. Charlie always supported Nicole and sent her to Green Valley. My son Kyle and Nicole were the same age, and they met at the school long before I knew who Charlie was.

After his divorce, Charlie poured himself into his work, his daughter, and the church. He says that when Nicole was just two years old, she asked him if they could go to church. Charlie agreed, stepped foot inside our church, and never looked back. I've often asked him, "What made you want to go to church?" He tells me that after his divorce, he realized that he didn't want to continue on with his partying lifestyle. He wanted to be an example for his daughter.

My mother, Carma, and Ken had always loved Charlie and kept inviting him to our family functions. For five years, Charlie and I dated, broke up, and then got back together. I was the one starting the break-up cycle all over again, but I think I broke up with Charlie because I was afraid. He seemed a bit untamed, and I didn't know if I could trust his heart, but I found that I couldn't live without my friend Charlie who had made his way into the hearts of my family long before me.

After breaking up with Charlie, he kept his distance, but my mother and sister still hadn't given up on us. A friend told me that Charlie was dating someone else from another church, and that I should really think about him again. I responded with, "How nice for him," but this new information really shook me up.

I did some serious praying and thinking about my life. My boys were older now, and seemed well adjusted. Would bringing someone into my life permanently be good for them? I struggled back and forth. I decided to meet with Charlie for coffee and give him my blessing, and basically just let him go.

"I think we have a future together."

We met for coffee a couple days before Valentine's Day, and I found out that he was planning to let me go as well. We would part as friends, and that would be that, but that's not exactly what happened. As I sat there and listened to him tell me about his new girlfriend, I think I saw Charlie the way God wanted me to see him: a faithful, committed friend who would always be loyal to me. God knew the future and knew that my family and I would need him in the years to come. Before I knew it, I blurted out, "I think we have a future together." Charlie gulped, his eyes widened. He looked shocked. *I* was shocked. Who said that?

This caused Charlie a lot of stress, as he had already ordered flowers for Valentine's Day to send to his girlfriend, but in his heart, as he has explained to me, I was always "the one". We parted and he promised to pray and see what God wanted him to do. I went home, shocked and confused. Had I just messed up my life? Had I just messed up *his* life? I talked to the Lord, I talked to my closest friends, and I talked to my sons. They liked Charlie, but they did not see him as stepfather material (not yet, anyway).

Charlie says that he went back to the florist and ordered a second bouquet of flowers to send to me. His friend who worked there grinned and raised her eyebrows at him. He blushed and paid for the flowers.

After about three days, Charlie called me and wanted to talk. He told me about a dream that he had. In his dream, an older pastor was telling the story about Abraham looking for wives for his sons in their own family. Charlie really believed that this dream was from the Lord and was directing him to find a wife in his own church family, and yes, that was me. So, here we were. What had I done? I had altered my life considerably. I had just prayed and surrendered my life to the Lord as a single person, giving up on marrying. I had been single for fourteen years and I was doing fine as a single mom; I had a good career, many friends, and was working hard in ministry. This would certainly rock the boat, and rock the boat, it did!

THE WEDDING

Journal Entry—July 4, 2001

> *"Do not fear disgrace, you will not be humil-*
> *iated. You will forget the shame of your youth and*
> *remember no more the reproach of your widow-*
> *hood... I will have compassion on you, says the Lord*
> *your redeemer" (Isaiah 54:4-8, NIV).*
>
> *How I have searched the Scriptures and prayed.*
> *What God has revealed to me through His incredi-*
> *ble grace and mercy is that He has forgiven my past*
> *completely. He views me as a deserted widow, and*
> *in His mercy and compassion, He has given me*
> *another chance to honor marriage vows.*
>
> *I want to be a good and loving wife to Charlie.*
> *I want to be the woman in Proverbs 31. I feel like*
> *God has given me such a gift in Charlie. He picked*
> *out someone for me that can understand me and*
> *love me for who I am.*

Charlie and I dated for one year, and boy did he pull out all the stops. He took my boys and me and his daughter Nicole to Disneyland. We went to the movies, bowling, and out to dinner, all in typical Charlie style. The boys started to really warm up to this new man in our lives. I think Charlie instinctively knew that to win my heart, he would need to win theirs first.

I would share details with my friends, Julie and Tami, as we ran together very early in the mornings. I wanted their blessing, and they were instrumental in helping me in the journey. I really struggled to let someone in my life and to give up control. I felt like this would be the most critical decision I had ever made in my whole life. It could alter our lives forever, good or bad.

"Cherished, Loved, Blessed."

The day came when Charlie approached my boys and asked them if he could marry their mother. After the year of fun-filled activities and trips, they heartily agreed.

My mother said it was about time, and all my friends and family agreed. I just had to get on board. I was still wrestling the old demons of my past, still trying to pull the labels off myself, but as I began to let God heal me and Charlie love me, the new labels started to appear: "Cherished, Loved, Blessed".

We were married in the summer of 2001. We invited the whole church, and our children were a huge part of the ceremony. I was thrilled to have our best friends Doug and Julie Titus stand up with us, as well as my siblings. Doug and Julie had been instrumental in supporting us in prayer. I don't know what I would have done without their love and support. It took real courage for them to stand by us and help us walk out our convictions. I think I was kind of living in a bubble, not realizing at first what was circulating around the church.

We found out that some people in the church did not agree with our marriage. We had both been married and divorced, and they felt that remarrying was not biblical. I cannot emphasize enough that

I didn't want to do anything that went against the Bible, and this caused me considerable distress. We prayed, we cried, we talked with our friends and family and we counseled with my Uncle Jim and Aunt Carol, who were pastoring in Roseville, California at the time. I felt like we were on the chopping block, ready to be beheaded. How in the world could what we felt like was God's calling and blessing be considered wrong?

It's quite sobering to realize that when you have ventured out into a journey, some of the people who you have held in the highest esteem have disapproved of your decision. It shakes you to your core, and I found myself in panic mode, struggling to hear from God—I mean *really* hear from God, like a "parting of the seas" kind of answer. That is where faith had to lead. I cannot explain how God answered, but He did. Through His Word, through people, and through the peace that He gave us in our journey, we felt like He placed His stamp of approval upon our union.

Our wedding day was beautiful. As my two sons walked me down the aisle towards my new life, I felt joy and excitement. At the same time, I thought of those dear ones who were not there, because they chose not to be, or felt like they could not be.

Rather than mourn over the few that were not there, I chose to rejoice with the ones who were. My mourning had certainly turned to rejoicing, and in my heart, I quickly asked God to comfort the ones that suffered in silence. I knew their hearts were not turned against me, and I had to trust God to do what only He could do in His time.

I will say, though, that I am grateful for that season. It caused us to dive deep into God's Word and into His heart for us, and even though it was our journey, it was everyone else's, too. In our hearts, we allowed those in our church family to go on their own journey. Both Charlie and I felt like it was each person's individual conviction in how they viewed the Scriptures. If they allowed us to pursue our journey, then we had to allow them to pursue theirs. What God showed us was His love, forgiveness, and unmerited favor. Yes, we both had failed marriages, but we both had walked out our singleness and our healing, and we felt like God was saying, "Now, walk out your new life in the blessing of marriage." I am so grateful to God for giving us Charlie. He was the answer to my heart's cry. I knew he would never leave me. He was committed and as determined as I was to have a successful and beautiful life. That would be the honeymoon stage. What was yet to come was real life.

CHAPTER EIGHT

A Blended Family

Journal Entry—October 10, 2001

> *God, stir up a passion in the lives of my family and in my own heart to serve You with abounding love and desire for Your Word and for Your presence.*

NICOLE

I didn't have a daughter until I married Nicole's father. She and Kyle were both fourteen when we married. Even though she went to the same school as my sons and we attended the same church, Nicole and I were strangers. I know she probably wondered who this blonde woman was that married her father. When we moved into our first home, Charlie and I agreed that it was best to not make too many changes in Nicole's life, so she continued to live with her mother and visited us every other weekend.

I truly regret that decision. I think it prolonged Nicole's ability to feel like an important part of our family. She had these new stepbrothers to compete with

"Through trial and error, we found our rhythm."

and I am sure that she missed her father, as his life had turned upside down. I was working full-time, trying to keep up with my teenage sons, and adapting to a new marriage after being single for so long.

It was a recipe for disaster, but through trial and error, we found our rhythm. It was wonderful to have a husband to establish a home with and to bring home a paycheck. We lived in the nicest home I had ever lived in. All was well, except for the beautiful brunette little girl, who kept her feelings to herself. I had no idea she was suffering inside, missing her dad and feeling displaced.

It all came out when her mother sued us for child support. It really did seem ridiculous, because Charlie had always provided for his daughter, and we wanted to take care of Nicole. It was at that time that Charlie quit his job because he was having pain in his back from an old injury. He was an electrician and was pursuing his real estate license, but at that time, child support was based on his income, which was no longer a factor. The court settled on a small monthly amount, but at the same time, we felt like we needed to have Nicole live with us full time, which she seemed excited to do.

I knew how to raise boys; most of the time, you just took them outside and pitched them a ball, but having a daughter—especially a teenaged daughter—was new to me. Both Nicole and I will tell you that it took some time, but we came to really love each other. She has called me her true mom. I am grateful that she has a good relationship with her own mom, and I have always tried to stay in my own lane, but Nicole has enough love for both of us, and I bring some different things to the table. My family embraced Nicole, and she became such a bright spot in our family. Her contagious laugh and funny sense of humor soon wound its way into our hearts.

Our new home in Aptos, just fifteen minutes from Watsonville, was an older home dated with wood paneling throughout the house, white carpeting upstairs and downstairs, and dark walnut cabinets in the kitchen. It had a huge brick fireplace in the living room with a hot tub on the deck. Kyle and Nicole were excited to move into their own rooms, and in the loft overlooking the living room was the guest room where we invited my mother to live. She was now babysitting full-time for Krista and no longer worked as a caregiver. I remember thinking that we were moving into a mansion. I had never lived in a house that big. After living there for one year, we were able to purchase the home. It was the first home Charlie and I had ever owned. It seemed like a million years since I had lived in "the bedroom".

ANNIE

Russ and Annie had just married and were happy to start their lives together. They were able to purchase a home in Brooksdale up in the Santa Cruz Mountains.

I just knew from the beginning when they first started dating that Annie had captured Russ' heart, and she captured mine as well. I loved her laugh, sense of humor, and, more importantly, her kind heart. I knew that she and I would be great friends. I was thrilled for my oldest son, especially after the painful breakup he experienced in high school.

Annie is from Indiana, and we met her family when they attended our church in Watsonville just after they moved to California. Some of the best Easters we've had as a family have been with her family. Her mother, father, and brothers often pulled out banjos and guitars, singing and swaying to country songs and hymns. Russ and Kyle would join in with their guitars and we would all swing in time to the music.

I remember their wedding and how handsome my son looked. I was so grateful to the Lord for blessing him with a wonderful wife. He had been through a lot being raised by a single mom, and I felt like God was giving him the desires of his heart.

Annie looked like a movie star to me, and when I danced with my son, it felt like a dream. It is in those moments that a whole lifetime can flash before your eyes. Here was this son of mine.

"Annie picked up where I left off. They made a home together and I could tell that they knew how to work things out."

Did I give him all that he needed? Did he know how to be a husband? Who in the world was his example? However, I didn't need to worry. Annie picked up where I had left off. They made a home together, and I could tell they knew how to work things out.

Both Kyle and Nicole attended high school at Monte Vista. We felt like we had twins. Their high school years were filled with proms, baseball games, driver's ed., and homework. I still worked full-time at Granite Construction, and Charlie was selling real estate and doing very well. We were still trying to find the rhythm of being married, as well as being stepparents. We had a few bumps and bruises along the way, mainly just trying to find our way.

Charlie was working on establishing his role as head of the house, and I struggled to relinquish it. After years of being single, I had become pretty independent. I loved having a husband to share the financial burden and someone to raise my sons with, but was reluctant to fully hand him the reins. This caused some tension in the house, especially when he would require the kids to do chores, clean up their rooms, and put their dishes in the dishwasher. Those seem like reasonable requests, but he began to sound like a dictator, and I strongly resisted, but some wise words from our counselors, some long-time friends of Charlie, really helped us figure out our rhythm. After losing my identity through divorce and having regained it, I was in no hurry to have my husband control everything about my life, but when we learned to hear each other and respect each other's point of view, we started making progress as a couple and as a family. Charlie stepped into his role as stepfather, and both of my boys respected him and appreciated him. Nicole and I had really developed our relationship and began to bond. We both knew that I could never replace her mother, nor did I want to. She had a solid, loving relationship with her mom that was more a friendship; I was the strict mom, the one she really respected, and was perhaps a bit afraid of.

Nicole met Ben Harris in one of her classes at Cabrillo College, and there was no turning back. They married soon after, with our blessing. Nicole's wedding day was especially wonderful for Charlie. He cried when he gave her away at the altar, and when he gave the toast at the reception, I remember thinking that it was a miracle that brought us to this day.

Our sweet little family seemed to be thriving, and it seemed like everything was working out perfectly; it would be smooth sailing from here.

CHAPTER NINE

Devestating News

Journal Entry—March 2004

> *"I would have lost heart unless I had believed that I would see the goodness of the Lord in the land of the living" (Psalm 27:13-14, NKJV).*

One evening, out of the blue, I received a phone call from Corcoran State Prison. My father had been transferred to that prison the year before, and I had only visited him once while he was there. The prison had a reputation of being one of the toughest prisons in California, and we had worried about my dad when he was sent there.

The person on the other end of the phone was the warden of the prison.

"Are you Rhonda Abellera?" he asked. It's a frightening thing to be called by the authorities; you don't know what they are going to say. "I'm calling to inform you that your father has died of a heart attack."

I felt my knees weaken as Charlie franticly asked, "What happened?"

"In everything give thanks, for this is the will of God in Christ Jesus concerning you."

"My dad is dead," I said, feeling like I also was dead inside.

The warden continued to explain that my dad had a heart attack while in his cell. From the phone calls we had received from my dad, we knew that the work they were assigning him to do was quite difficult for a sixty-five-year-old man. He told us that he could barely keep up and often was gasping for breath and had to rest as he finished cleaning the lunchroom.

I called my sisters, my brother, and my mom, who had since moved in to live with her good friend. His death hit us like a ton of bricks. So that was it; this was the end of his life? How could his life be over?

As a family, we were stunned. I called my Uncle Jim and Aunt Carol. All he said to me was, "Don't worry, I'll handle everything,"— and they did. They made arrangements for his body and planned the funeral.

I had no idea what you did with a body. We wanted an open casket because it's hard to bury someone you haven't seen in a long time. We just needed to be able to say goodbye to him.

The funeral was in Roseville, CA where his parents were buried, because we didn't want to bring attention to his passing. It was just our family and a sprinkling of a few friends. That was enough. He didn't really look like the dad of my childhood. You could tell that his life's journey had been hard on him.

We said kind words about him. Russ and Kyle sang a song over his casket. We wept over him and his life. Then we said goodbye.

It was a few days later that my mom received some letters from some of the inmates that knew him. We found out that he had died in his cell, singing a new worship song that he had written: "In everything give thanks, in everything give thanks, for this is the will of God in Christ Jesus concerning you." He died in the arms of his cellmate, and his cellmate sent my mother the lyrics to his song. I tried to picture my father singing this song, even though I had no idea of what the tune was.

There were other letters that told how my father had encouraged many of the men and helped them find the Lord. These words brought sweet redemption to our hearts. The Lord had truly rescued my dad and restored him. As much as our hearts were sad, we knew that we would see my dad again in heaven, dressed in white, without his denim prison clothes.

CHAPTER TEN

─•─────•─────•─

Becoming Grandparents

T he wonderful thing about life is that on the heels of sorrows come unexpected joys. We soon discovered that we would be grandparents. Russ and Annie were expecting! They had revealed the news on a family vacation in Hawaii. I was overjoyed to take on the new role as a grandmother. I dreamed of what that dear grandchild would call me. I practiced many names, only to find out that the grandchildren pick the name, but I really didn't care what they called me!

On January 5, 2006, I received the call that Annie was in labor, so Charlie and I dropped what we were doing and headed to the hospital. I discovered all of Annie's large family in the waiting room. I was ushered into the delivery room along with her mom, sisters, and a couple friends. After several hours, I remember in particular that it seemed like the labor had stopped. The epidural

"On the heels of sorrow come unexpected joy."

was wearing off, and Annie was in extreme pain. "Pray," her mother shouted, and we all started to pray. I looked across the room, and behind the curtain stood her sweet father leaning against the wall. His eyes were shut, but his face was contorted and he looked like he himself was in pain. Finally, we heard his loud, screaming cry, which let us know the baby had arrived! Very quickly, we all left to wait in the waiting room. After a few minutes, Russ called us back into the room, and exclaimed, "His name is Russell Don." We all cheered! I couldn't have been happier to have another Russell in my life.

I stepped into the role of a grandmother as naturally as I did a mother, unlike Charlie, who seemed to take some time soaking it all in. No doubt the adjustment of being a grandfather was a process, just like becoming a stepfather. I remember saying to him, "Charlie, you are now a grandfather; you have to step into that role with me." Something in him snapped to attention, and from that moment on, he embraced that grandbaby. This was not a step-grandchild, this was his grandchild.

RUSSELL

Russ called me that afternoon and told me to come up to the hospital. When I arrived, Annie was sleeping and Russ was rocking his new baby. He gestured for me to come over and he placed the baby in my arms. I sat in the rocker, and there I rocked that sweet grandson for the first time. Russ and I just looked at each other and grinned. Here I sat, rocking my firstborn's firstborn. How differently life had turned out. I remembered the first time I had held Russ in my arms. The circumstances were quite different. I could have never imagined the blessing that would have followed, but God did.

Russell, my first grandchild, is the one that unlocked the section in my heart that I never knew existed. I dearly love my family, but it was this grandchild that brought extreme joy and happiness into my life. He loves to sketch and draw and was practically born with a pencil in his hand. I remember trying to learn how to draw Larry the Cucumber and Bob the Tomato from the cartoon *Veggie Tales*. I soon mastered it as two-year-old Russell eagerly coached me.

This grandson is dark haired with big brown eyes like his mother, and he has developed a very sophisticated sense of humor. Even as he grows into a teenager, I still feel a special bond that he and I have shared ever since I first sat and rocked him in the hospital.

EVERETT

Everett Riley was born on November 19, 2009. I remember taking his big brother Russell to the hospital to meet him. Russell enjoyed meeting his new brother, but sincerely questioned his parents about him, such as, "Is he going to live with us? Do we love him?" Everett was a calm baby and didn't have colic like his brother. Everett soon joined "Mimi Day", and I remember Annie strapping him on to me with his baby wrap and waving good-bye as she walked out the door. Everett was as happy as a lark being so close to his Mimi, but sooner or later I would have to unstrap him and spend some time with Russell. He demanded equal time and wondered when we could send Everett back to the hospital.

I loved playing with those two little boys. As a single mom, I didn't get to stay home with my boys, but now, with my new schedule, I relished my time with the boys. We built forts, we took walks, and we watched *Thomas the Tank Engine.*

Everett developed an English accent when he was young, and I would listen to him tell me about things from the wealth of knowledge in his young mind. Everett loves building LEGOs, learning things, the outdoors, fly-fishing, and is interested in anything you want to talk about.

Russ had just started with the Sheriff's Department in Santa Cruz County in 2008, and they had sold their home in Brooksdale. They wanted to get a bigger house closer to town and approached us about moving in with us for a year to save for a down payment. We were empty-nesters, as Kyle and Nicole had moved out earlier and now we were faced with a very big empty home.

I was thrilled with the thought of tucking my grandsons in at night and having some little people around the house full-time. Our home soon became a very busy place as we began shuffling furniture and rearranging rooms to accommodate our new tenants.

I made a deal with Annie. I would clean the house and the kitchen if she would shop and prepare the meals. I turned the cooking over to her, and I think we made a great team. Many times, in the evening, as Charlie and I would clean up the kitchen, we would hear Russ and Annie playing with the boys outside. It reminded me of what my mom had done for me with my two boys.

ROSIE

Russ and Annie moved out of our house after one year when they found a home to purchase, and they were excited to move for many reasons, mainly because they were pregnant with their third baby! They moved into a cute little home in town that was in the heart of Watsonville. On December 9, 2011, our sweet granddaughter, Rosalee Mae, was born. She captured the heart of this Mimi. I took care of her older brothers while their mom and dad were at the hospital. I took the excited brothers to meet their new baby sister, and when we arrived, they were enamored with their new sister. Everett looked at me and said, "You can pet him."

Everett's best buddy is Rosie. When she was just two years old, I could hear Everett directing her on making muffins in their mud kitchen outside my window. She would respond in her English accent, because it was Everett who taught her how to talk.

Rosie is a girl after my own heart. She has a horse named Dandy and knows how to ride him. She adores her animals and outdoors. She helps around the kitchen and knows her way around most anything. She has her dad's sense of humor, especially when she wrinkles up her nose and laughs. Her long blond hair flows through the wind when she runs, just like mine did when I was a young girl. You can tell she belongs to me; my "mini me". She is a strong girl like her mamma and is not afraid to tackle any challenge. She is always so full of ideas; she shakes her head, holds up her hands, and says, "Mimi, you're gonna love it." We fell in love with that little granddaughter, and I have been so grateful that the Lord gave me a little girl to love.

CHAPTER ELEVEN

New Adventures

Journal Entry—January 3, 2009

New life, new adventures. I'm excited to see God's plan unfold in my life. I will face challenges, but I know that I can do all things through Christ who strengthens me.

It was 2008, and the market had taken a huge downturn. After working at Granite Construction for almost twenty years, they began to downsize and encouraged long-term employees to take a severance package. I was tired of working full-time and ended my employment in September 2008. I wanted to fully embrace my new role as a grandmother. It was heartbreaking to leave my friends, especially my boss, Tracy, who had poured into me and had given me a brand-new promotion. Even though it was short-lived, I relished my time with her. As I packed up my things in the proverbial "box", I walked through the halls alone. Everyone else in my department was at the company picnic, and we had already said our goodbyes. It was hard to believe that I was leaving; I had such mixed feelings: anticipation of a new season in my life, but a sadness and uncertainty of what the future would hold.

I embraced my new role as a grandmother and welcomed the free time to start our official "Mimi Days".

We eventually had to short sell our beautiful home, and I was sad to let it go. This is where I had tucked my grandbabies into bed, and where I had hosted many family barbecues and parties, but I was ready for the next season of our lives.

THE PHILIPPINES TRIP

When I married Charlie, I knew that he loved to go on mission trips around the world. He had traveled to many countries with our missions team from our church, but I had never gone on a trip. It is not that I didn't ever think about it, but I mostly had to focus on work and my boys, and I had always thought that my first trip abroad would be to Paris. So, when Charlie asked me to go with him to the Philippines, I felt like I needed to go.

As I tell this story, I feel a bit like a wimp. I've always thought of myself as a pretty spiritually strong woman. After what I have been through in life, I felt like nothing could shake me, but I was wrong. This trip shook me to my bones.

In January 2011, we traveled to San Francisco with our team and boarded a flight on China Air at 12:00 midnight. We arrived first in Taiwan after fourteen hours of flight, and then we flew to Manila.

Missionaries Mark and Sarah Brown picked us up at the airport and we piled into two vans. The girls and I rode with Sarah and Charlie, and the other men in our group rode with Mark. We weaved in and out of traffic; there were no rules, no speed limits—just honk your horn and drive.

Suddenly, a siren startled us, and with a loud megaphone, we were told to pull over. The men in the other van continued on their way as we were pulled over by the side of the road. The officer began to talk to the driver in the Tagalog language. Sarah began to join in. Apparently, the officer wanted to be paid to let us go. Sarah was adamant that the driver did not give in to the bribe. I was shocked as I saw the officer pull out a machine gun and ask the driver to get out of the van. Sarah frantically tried to call Mark, but they were too far down the freeway. I began to wonder if this would be my first and last day in the Philippines. I had heard stories about kidnaping tourists, especially blonde ones, and especially women. Finally, after much yelling and dealing, the officer was paid, and we were allowed to leave.

Mark and Sarah serve in the heart of the city of Manila and minister to the children and their families. We came to help with the Vacation Bible School (VBS) that they would have during the next week.

The most dramatic of movie sets could not begin to capture the poverty and despair these people live in. There were children everywhere running through the streets. I don't know how they didn't get hit by the jeepneys and motorcycles that weaved through the traffic.

That first morning, we went into the outdoor market in downtown Manila to buy supplies. We were literally running to try and keep up with our guide, dodging the merchants, dogs, roosters, and people and trying not to get run over by the hundreds of vehicles weaving in and out.

I felt like I was on the set of the movie *Slumdog Millionaire*, or so it seemed. We went down by the water, and I stepped over three small children, maybe nine months to two years old. They were naked, crying, and all alone. We had to step over them in order to continue on our way. I could not reconcile my feelings or emotions. Each day of the trip brought new feelings, situations, and experiences to deal with.

Saturday, we did an outreach down the road and into the streets. The neighborhood children came and surrounded us. They were a bit shy toward the visitors, as we were called. They were particularly interested in me, the blonde visitor. They would run their hands through my hair and chatter to one another. I didn't understand them, but I heard the word "angel".

We sang songs, bandaged wounds, and gave them the biggest smiles we had. That afternoon, we visited the children in their neighborhoods and invited them to the VBS the following week. We were invited into a couple homes, where they served Sprite and crackers. I was told by my team to eat whatever they offered you because it was a big sacrifice to offer you something. There was also a pig tied up outside on the front porch (I think he was the next day's dinner).

It was getting dark, and Jessna, one of the workers in the church, suggested that we ride a tricycle back to the church. I hesitated, as I had seen how those things just flew by the cars with people hanging on for dear life. However, I was tired, so I agreed. A man stopped for us and she said, "Get in." I asked her, "Are you coming?" She climbed in after me, much to my relief. It seemed like we drove for miles; I had no idea where he was taking us. Nothing looked familiar. I looked down at the floorboards, but there weren't any, just the payment below that we were driving over. Where was my husband? Why did he leave me on my own like this?

We started VBS on Monday, and I was assigned with another young girl from our team to teach the lessons. We walked down the street into a courtyard to set up our station. We would be telling the story to six different groups with an interpreter, something I had never done before. It would be a very long day. The other stations, crafts, and games were across the street in a large basketball court. I wouldn't see Charlie until lunch time. He was always surrounded by children. They were riding on his back, laughing as he teased them. He was certainly in his element. Since I had married him, I had never seen him so alive and excited. I was glad that I had come.

We averaged about 400 children a day. The more I told the stories and saw their faces, the more I fell in love with these children. I no longer turned away when they ran their fingers through my hair. Instead, I turned and hugged them. Their bright eyes and smiles made a permanent impression on me. I realized why I had come: to share the love of Jesus and to get over myself.

TEEN CHALLENGE

Journal Entry—January 17, 2011

Lord Jesus, I am so grateful for Your love and grace to me. Thank You for the opportunity You've given me at Teen Challenge. I am so hon-

ored by the love, affection, and anticipation of the women. I must cling to You and hold on tightly.

When I returned from my Philippines adventure, I was contacted by Melissa, the director at the ladies' Teen Challenge in Watsonville, a Christian drug and alcohol rehabilitation program for women. I had met her several months earlier as my friend and running buddy Tami Noonan and I went weekly to conduct a Bible study for the ladies. We loved our time with the ladies and it was a wonderful experience that we shared together.

However, the call from the director was something I did not expect.

"I have your office ready," she said.

"What, my office?" I responded.

"Yes, you're my new Assistant Director."

I was stunned; I didn't expect this. "Well, I'll have to pray about it," I said. Isn't that what you're supposed to say?

I accepted the position after one day of prayer and started a journey that would again shake me to my bones. I didn't really feel like I had any qualifications, but I was willing to learn. Upon my first day, it felt like a firehose of information and experiences. I already knew the ladies, and they seemed happy that I had come on board, but coming once a week for a Bible study is very different than being on staff.

Showing up once a week, I could love on them, hear their stories, and pray with them. Being on staff, I had to discipline them, organize their day, and keep them on task, something that was much harder to do. It wasn't in my nature to be strict with them, and I struggled at first.

I was also expected to counsel with them individually. My first counseling session was a bit of a shock to me. I was raised in church all my life and had served in many capacities, including worship team, choir, and small group leader, but these "qualifications" only went so far.

I arranged my office so that it was comfortable for my counseling session and practical for all the paperwork that I had. My folders were neatly put away, my pens and pencils arranged around my computer, and my desk lamp and pictures were nicely displayed. I was ready.

The knock on my door was loud and forceful. "Come in," I said, excited for my first counselee.

The door opened, and what appeared like a raging bull was a young woman who was about twenty-six years old, dressed in dirty sweats with a hoodie pulled over her colored red hair. Her name was Kelly, and her blue eyes glared at me as she slumped down into the chair.

"Hello Kelly, I'm so happy to be working with you today. Now, I'll just start by asking you a few questions. Can you tell me why you're here?" I asked.

"Of course. I'm a stumbling drunk, no one wants me around, and I don't want to be here," she replied.

The string of curses and language rolled out of her mouth like a waterfall. She uttered things I had never heard of.

"Now Kelly, you know that Jesus loves you and—"

"That's the last thing I want to hear about! I've been down that road before, and no priest wants to hear what I've done."

It was at that moment that I realized I was not prepared for this job. I would need to draw from God's help if I was going to survive. After that first experience, each morning, I would ask God to help me and show me how to love these women.

"I began to see the miracle working power of Jesus transforming their lives. All I had to do was love them."

The weeks went on, and with Melissa's guidance, I began to grow in my role. I still struggled in trying to connect with the ladies, until one Monday night when I was leading the Bible study.

They continued to call me a "Barbie doll". They thought I was someone who had no idea what she was talking about, a "goody two-shoes".

I pulled from the experiences that have shaped my life and began to tell them about my father, who served time in prison. As my story unfolded, I told them of the shame and suffering we endured as a family as he was arrested and taken to prison. I also shared how my husband of nine years had left me with a small boy and a baby on the way.

Something shifted in them. I, too, knew so much pain. One by one, the ladies started sharing their stories. I began to realize that I was like them, in a way. We all had been traumatized by circumstances and events in our lives. We were all on the same playing field; we all had endured a tremendous amount of pain. We all needed the healing power of Jesus in our lives. Once I realized that I couldn't save them or heal them, I began to see the miracle-working power of Jesus transform their lives. All I had to do was love them.

CHAPTER TWELVE

The Move To Bend

Journal Entry—October 8, 2014

> *Lord, establish my steps and the steps of my family. Help me to partner with You and believe in the unseen work of Your hand.*

I watched the car disappear down the road early that final morning that carried my son Russ, daughter-in-law Annie, and my three grandchildren, who were on their way to a new life in Bend, Oregon.

I hugged the children goodbye, choking back the tears, knowing it was only for a few weeks before I would see them again, but Rosie was just two years old; a few weeks would seem like years. I looked Annie in the eye and we both turned away, knowing that the separation would also be hard on us. I knew that we would be joining them in December, but it seemed like forever.

I had never even thought about moving until Russ and Annie started talking to us about it. They both said that they wouldn't move unless we went with them. I realized the magnitude of our decision. If we stayed, they would stay and possibly give up their dreams. If we all agreed to go, then what would this move hold for Charlie and I?

Charlie and I were born and raised in Watsonville and we had raised our children there. I thought about the lifelong friends I had made and all the life we had done together. My close friends, my tribe, had witnessed and walked with me through many traumas in my life, and I had witnessed many of their life's traumas. We carried each other through thick and thin, and they were my extended family.

The hardest part was leaving my mom. Ken and Carma had moved to Redding several years earlier, and now, only my sister Krista and brother Brad (who had moved back to the states) were in town close to her. I felt responsible for her. I also struggled with leaving Kyle in San Francisco and Ben and Nicole in Santa Cruz, but they were young adults now with lives of their own. Kyle was established in San Francisco, writing music and singing his songs.

I thought about my grandchildren. I would have to choose them and leave the others or choose the others and leave them. This is where the trust came. I had to believe that God was directing our steps.

It had only been about six months since we all had decided to pick up our lives and go on a new adventure. We had just moved next door to Russ and Annie after moving out of our big home in Aptos. With the real estate crash of 2008, we had to short sell our home, and after about two years of trying to renegotiate our loan with the bank to no avail, we moved in 2012.

Our vision to move all started in the summer of 2014 after vacationing with Russ and Annie in Bend. They began to talk about moving and asked us if we could consider moving to Bend with them. They were looking for a place to raise their children in a more rural community that was more family-oriented.

Russ initially applied to the Bend Police Department and found out there were no openings, but before we could drive back home from vacation, he had an interview scheduled. From there, the journey began. Charlie, who always seems to have a sense of what direction to take, applied for his broker's license in Oregon, knowing that he would need it when we moved. I had a feeling we

"Sometimes God takes people out of your life, only to weave them right back in when you need them the most."

84

would move, but was thinking it would take a couple of years. I had time to adjust to the idea.

It all happened so fast that I think my family and friends could barely believe we were moving away. There were a lot of tears and a lot of "we'll stay in touch" moments, but in reality, when you pick up one life and head towards a new one, you leave some things and people behind. It took me a while to emotionally release the previous life and embrace the new one.

I prayed a lot during those months, and God began to confirm to us that this was His plan. Russ got hired on at the Bend Police Department; he started work in September and bought a home for his family.

We packed up our home and planned to move, but we still had no house to move into and no jobs in Oregon. I wouldn't ordinarily recommend moving when you don't have a home to move into or a job, but in this case, I somehow knew that God was asking us to take the next few steps. It is easy to say that God will show you what to do, but to actually walk it out takes a lot of courage and faith. The home we had purchased closed exactly on December 5th, the day before we moved to Bend.

Sometimes, God takes people out of your life only to weave them right back in when you need them the most. Uncle Jim and Aunt Carol had moved to Bend about five years prior and were strategic in our plan to move. Reuniting with them after all they had meant to our family was an extra blessing. We started attending their church and were also excited to connect again with Mike and Kim Alexander, our cousins. God also brought another crucial friend back into my life: my childhood friend Dianna Salciccoli. I met her for coffee during our vacation and she seemed excited that we might move to Bend. We hadn't seen each other in over twenty-five years and were excited to catch up. We both were grandmothers now, and it seemed like another piece was added to the puzzle. I was certain that this was God's plan for our lives.

I still remember how it felt to drive up to Russ and Annie's new house in Bend in the loaded-up truck with all our earthly possessions. It was early December, and there was a dusting of snow on the ground. The kids weren't home, but knew that we would be pulling up at any time, so they left the door unlocked. I guess you can do that in Bend.

It felt so magical walking into their sprawling home with two lit Christmas trees and Christmas decorations all over the house. There were drawings and artwork on the fridge and Christmas presents under the tree. The sound of steps and laughter came from the garage, and I turned to see Russell and Everett bounding up the stairs with Rosie following. All three came running and jumped into my arms. Yes, this is why I had moved. I was once again home.

CHAPTER THIRTEEN

Two Little Boys, Two Wonderful Men

KYLE

I often think about those years when my life fell apart: how I worried about my boys, who they would be, what would they do, and who would they become. If I could have known then what I know and have experienced now, I'm not sure that knowing the things that have happened would have been an advantage. I'm pretty certain that it was better not knowing and instead just trusting God in the storms and listening for His whisper.

I had to do a lot of trusting God and just powering through life, as difficult as it was at times.

I can still see that trooper, loaded up with all his earthly belongings, headed down the driveway to start his new life at twenty years of age. Throughout his life, Kyle and I have always been close. Even though sometimes he was a rascal during his toddler years, he was a blessing as a teenager. I cried a million tears that day. This was the boy that I had put on a cape

> *"I'm pretty certain that it was better not knowing, and just trusting God in the storms, listening for His whisper."*

and flown around the backyard with. When he was little, Russ and I had to pretend we were the Batmobile chasing the Joker so that Kyle wouldn't cry in the car. This season of my life was over. I was an empty-nester. I was done raising boys. I didn't think this day would come, and I wasn't ready for it.

Kyle later moved to San Francisco, and through those years, he went through some heartbreaks. It is hard to watch your children suffer. It is even harder when you try to find a reason; maybe because I was a single mom when I raised him, or maybe because he felt rejected by his father. Regardless of the reason, I began to reach out to Kyle to find some common ground on which we could be buddies again. I missed my sidekick, especially after his brother had married.

He started playing the guitar at thirteen, and it has never left his hands. He is a talented songwriter who writes about things that he cares about. His storytelling ability in his songs along with his free and easy style is masterful. He is like a modern-day Psalmist, expressing his heart and singing about his joys and sorrows. I can still hear his smooth, glassy voice and see the tilt of his head as he sings from his heart. Regardless of the message or the lyrics, his songs fill my heart with so much thankfulness that this is my son. I am his mom and I had the privilege of raising him.

Kyle and I are known for our long, heart-to-heart talks. When he was in high school, we'd stay up late and discuss his life. I don't know that we came to any conclusions, but I always told him that God had uniquely created him and loved him.

Kyle came to live in Bend one summer, and we spent many hours walking the river trail and just talking. We had only two rules: one, we could each express ourselves without judgement, and two, we would listen to each other without judgement. It is incredible to me that although we can be at polar opposites on a topic, we can still discuss and appreciate each other's point of view. He is still that funny, bright-eyed boy that saved my life that very special day in June.

RUSS

Journal Entry—March 14, 2020

Today is "Mimi Day". Lord, bless my sweet grandkids today and give us a good day.

I smile as I remember those two young sons that used to beg me to pitch a ball to them. I would have never dreamed that I would be a grandmother, enjoying my darling grandchildren.

Friday is the day I pick up the grandkids and bring them home for the entire day. I started "Mimi Day" when my first grandchild Russell was born, and then, as Everett and Rosie came along, I added them to our day, even when they were babies. I'd stock up on snacks and plan our day. Sometimes, we go on a walk or go to the Family Fun Center and play video games or go bowling. We always watch a movie, and they will always play with LEGOs or put on a puppet show. I think "Mimi Day" definitely has a dual purpose: to give mom a break and a day to catch up and to give me time with my grandchildren.

It's a day that we all look forward to. As they have grown up, I continue to enjoy our conversations and our time together. I often ask them if they will still come for "Mimi Day" when they are teenagers; so far, they have all said a resounding "yes".

"Sometimes you don't know what you are teaching your children, but they are always watching."

Many times, after "Mimi Day" is over, I'll take them to their father's police station instead of driving all the way back home, which is the midway point from their house.

Russ, who is now a police detective, will meet us at the front. He'll come out of the building just as the children pile out of the car with their backpacks and works of art that they have made for their parents. Rosie is usually the first one to run up into his arms as he laughs, but the boys will follow close behind.

I'm so proud of Russ. He doesn't have to be doing anything special, but he'll look at me, I'll look at him, and we'll share moments that have no meaning to anyone else but us. That sideways grin always melts my heart. He doesn't always say a lot, but whenever he sees me, he hugs me tightly.

He enjoys his children, and together, we enjoy them. So many things are unspoken, but we understand. We have a long history of loving each other. He will hug his children as they start telling him about their day, and then he'll wave goodbye to me as I drive off. The children are delighted to see their dad at work. Their big strong dad, tall like his father, is their defender and their provider, and he loves them passionately.

I remember when Russ first joined the Sheriff's Department in Santa Cruz County, I was very proud of this young man whom I had raised. How did he get tough enough to do this job? I stepped up my prayers for him to include his safety. His cool, calm demeaner serves him well.

So many times, I thought about the trauma of his childhood. I thought that not being raised in a home with two parents would ruin him. I've often asked him, "How in the world did you learn how to be such a good father?" He would say, "You taught me." Sometimes, you don't know what you are teaching your children, but they are always watching.

CHAPTER FOURTEEN

Life On The Farm

Journal Entry—April 23, 2020

I am so blessed by the people in my life and all the things God has blessed me with. So much of my family, mom, Krista and her family, my cousin Carmine, and Ben and Nicole now all live in central Oregon. We enjoy teas, hikes, and just getting together for "Taco Sunday".

It was a typical day in the summer as I stopped by Russ and Annie's farmhouse on the east side of town to see their new baby goat. Everett was going to sell this goat at the fair this year. Rosie was going to show her rabbit. The kids had joined 4-H, all except Russell. He doesn't like barnyard animals and prefers to draw, much like my brother Brad, who was a cartoonist growing up.

A slight breeze blew as the horses in their corral softly nickered. They thought I was coming to feed them. Bentley, the family dog, barked his welcome, and the cats also came to greet me.

What struck me that day as I walked into their home was the peaceful humming of the activity of a homeschool day. The feeling in their home reflected Annie's easy, no-nonsense style. She is fun and loving with her children and allows them to be brave and try new things, but she doesn't pull any punches when it comes to discipline. The children respect and love her dearly.

Rosie was at the table, coloring an assignment, Everett was quietly sitting on the couch reading, and Russell was in his room working on math. Annie was in the kitchen stirring up something yummy.

Annie was working on a new pie recipe to sell at the marketplace on the west side of town. There, she'd take her "Farmhouse Pie" trailer and set it up next to the other food trucks lined up in the streets. At this market, all the local vendors came out to sell their organic, homemade, and homegrown wares.

It had become a new tradition in our family to go out and help make pies. My mother and cousin Carmine came out to cut up apples and enjoy the sights and smells of a busy kitchen. Another pie came out of the oven, and I was hoping I would get to sample.

I sometimes help with pie-making, but that is not my forte; I'm better at playing with grandkids. On Fridays, I pick them up and take them home with me. They have special things that they like to do at my house: mainly eat snacks and watch their favorite cartoons. I love the noise; I love the mess. It reminds me of my two little boys who shared the back bedroom of my mother's house.

CHAPTER FIFTEEN

Walking In Forgiveness

Journal Entry—July 31, 2020

> *"I will do a new thing in your life: I will redeem the lost and restore what has been taken away. My promises will pass through the many generations of your life and of your family."*
>
> *It takes a lot of courage to explore your past and remember the pain as well as the wonderful things that have happened along the way, but that's what life is: loving life, loving family, and enduring the trauma and healing from the pain. God weaves together all those things through the tapestry of your life.*

For me, it took a lifetime to feel completely released from the pain of rejection and abandonment. My suffering didn't have to last that long, and it probably wouldn't have had it not been for the things that kept happening, but looking back, I can now see how God carefully orchestrated the events of my life.

While in the midst of settling my aunt's estate, my friend Dianna asked me if I wanted to work part-time in their new coaching firm that she and her husband Greg had started a few years back. After praying about it, I started working part-time in their office here in Bend. After being surrounded in an atmosphere of growth and healing, I knew that I wanted to became a life coach. I could certainly help other people walk out their lives of pain and into freedom because of all that I have been through. I am so grateful for Greg and Dianna's encouragement to pursue that calling in my life.

What I have found out is that unforgiveness and pain are like magnets. They attract new pain and new rejection. The rejection of my husband had created a trophy room of hurt and unforgiveness. When my father was convicted and went to prison, I added that pain to my trophy room. When I was rejected by my boss at work, friends, or family, that, too was added to my special room. Left to itself, this trophy room had grown into a tomb of remembrance. There, I would frequently visit and remember all the wrongs that had been done to me. I could recount years of conversation and actions associated with those wrongs.

What made matters worse was I then applied those wrongs to new people and to my new husband. When I didn't feel enough love or felt rejected, I was tempted to add the wrong I felt from Charlie to that trophy room. That certainly did not help my new marriage; in fact, I began to wonder if I had made a mistake. What had I gotten myself into?

They say that pain is a gift. I guess it is. If you didn't feel pain when you stubbed your toe, you could permanently injure your foot by not addressing the wound. That's what I was doing. I was walking around on injured feet, adding more wounds and injuries to my heart. It began to affect my emotions, and I felt like I was out of control. The more out-of-control I felt, the more I tried to control people and situations, until finally, I was exhausted.

I was aware of the harboring wounds festering in my heart early on, and I knew that I did not want to transfer them to my sons. I never wanted them to go through the pain of rejection like I had. I worked hard to be okay, but left on my own, I could never fully recover.

I would have continued walking around like that if it hadn't been for that pivotal weekend in San Francisco in 2010, where my sister Carma and her husband Ken had invited me to a special conference. There, we would hear a speaker who had been a career criminal for most of her life, but while in prison, God had healed and delivered her. From there, she started her ministry of deliverance. What grabbed me that day was her message of "soul wounds". I felt like she was talking about me. I went home that night and was determined to seek healing for my soul. I'd like to say that I immediately felt healed from the pain and unforgiveness that I was carrying around, but it has been a process.

It's impossible to completely explain the whole process, because it has taken many years. I was willing to invest the time in order to feel whole again.

I began to turn on worship music and just spend time in the presence of the Lord. It really took some discipline, because anytime you do that, you can get so distracted. It took repentance and an acknowledgement and welcoming of God's healing power, but the more time I spent, the more freedom I began to feel and the more I could release the pain I had been carrying for years. The painful memories of the past began to change, and I began to feel them and understand them through God's eyes. The Psalms were especially comforting to me. I felt the Word of God pour over me like oil. It bathed my soul and flushed out the pain.

The healing also started to affect my mind. I noticed that I started thinking differently about my ex-husband. I realized that God loved him and had a plan for his life. I began to pray for him, something that I had never done before. I also began to view my father differently. I feel like God gave me a new love for him. I began to feel compassion for the years he was walking in a living hell, trying to get free from the bondage that enslaved him. I would reread his letters, which I had barely read before and would usually just put away in a drawer, but when I began to really read them and understand his heart, I realized the deliverance he experienced in prison. He truly and remarkably had met the Lord in a real way. He died singing a worship song that I am sure escorted him into the presence of Jesus.

I love this new journey of living pain-free. In my mind, I could see myself taking a sledgehammer and knocking down the walls of that room of remembrance. Anytime I was tempted to add a new trophy to that room, I would take it to the Lord and let Him again heal the hurt that had invaded my heart.

Another important piece of this journey was understanding God's role in my pain. Unforgiveness is like an emotional prison that keeps us in bondage. We think that we are hurting the other person by not forgiving them, but in reality, we are hurting ourselves. By forgiving them, we are releasing them from our courtroom and walking away from a debt that we can't possibly carry. We then can let God be the judge and jury. He alone knows what we have suffered, and not only that, He knows what they have done to us. He will sort it all out. That revelation brought such freedom to me!

Because of that, I was able to develop a pretty civil relationship with my ex-husband and his wife. I was thankful for her for taking care of my boys when they were in their home. We've learned how to raise our boys together. There have been many graduations, birthday parties, and grandchildren that we have shared. I believe we genuinely care about each other and want the best for each other's lives. Beth Moore says, "Compassion is the key that unlocks forgiveness." Once I started praying for my ex-husband and his wife, I began to realize how important it was that we all loved our children and grandchildren together.

> *"Compassion is the key that unlocks forgiveness."*

As I look back at my father's life and all that had happened to him, I can reframe the terrible things that had happened to him and to my family. I can begin to be thankful that my father had gone to prison. I know that can seem so harsh, but I truly believe that was the only way God could get to his heart.

I am so deeply thankful for the care that the Lord showed my mother and how He protected her throughout the years. She would tell you that she has reaped the blessing of the Lord and His favor.

In looking back, I have gained a perspective that I could only have from living out my life. Through the many circumstances, good or bad, I can see the thread of God's grace, mercy, and love weaving through every trauma, every situation, and every person in my life.

His whispers to me through every storm became the bedrock of my faith. No matter what I went through, I could count on Jesus guiding me through the storms like He did in the picture I saw in my childhood.

I wouldn't trade the storms I've had for anything, because with them came the most incredible experiences and blessings that I could ever imagine. How He has guided and healed in the past gives me hope and faith for the future. I am grateful to know Jesus through my sufferings and through the power of His resurrection.

ENDNOTES

[1] Chapter One, page 10, "*The Lord's Prayer.*" Songwriter: Malotte, Albert Hay 1935

[2] Chapter One, page 11, "*You decorated my life.*" Songwriters: Hupp, Debbie and Morrison, Bob 1979

[3] Scripture Translations: (NKJV) New King James Version

[4] Scripture Translations: (NIV) New International Version

ENDORSEMENTS

Rhonda is an author who writes from the heart. Having had the privilege of watching her life story unfold, I can say that she honestly expresses her pain and triumphs in its raw truth. Rhonda's words will inspire hope for those who have traveled a rugged road.

—Dianna Salciccioli,
Coachwell Executive Coach

Rhonda's story is a moving—and sometimes raw—look at an ordinary girl becoming an extraordinary woman of faith. She testifies to God's absolute faithfulness and joyful reward.

—Carma Hunter

Rhonda gently holds the reader's hand through an honest and frank narrative of very painful, sensitive issues that leads to a conclusion of healing and restoration.

—Brad Bauer

Rhonda's story is inspirational and reminds us that God has a beautiful plan for our lives. Her story brought laughter, tears, warmth, and love to my heart.

—Krista Ross

Russell and Kyle

Me and my two sons

Our blended family

Russell and Kyle

Charlie and I with Russ and his family

My sisters and I with our husbands

My mom with her four kids

My two wonderful sons

Charlie and I on our wedding day

Ben and Nicole

My son Kyle the musician

Charlie and I with our dog Sophie in Bend

Fun with grandkids along the Deschutes River

Annie and my mom baking pies

Charlie and I with our grandkids along the snowy Deschutes River

White water along the Deschutes River

Breakthrough in a storm

ABOUT THE AUTHOR

Rhonda Abellera is a leadership coach in Bend, Oregon who specializes in coaching women to find their purpose and passion. She has served and worked with many teams and groups focused on caring and mentoring people in various walks of life. She is passionate about encouraging others with her story of redemption.